Treasured
Recipes
from the
Shipwreck
Coast

by Jan M. Holt

Illustrations by
David Conklin & Claudia Lewinski

This cookbook is a collection of favorite recipes,
which are not necessarily original recipes.

Published by Great Lakes Historical Society, Inc.

Library of Congress Number: 96-085091
ISBN: 0-9651844-0-4

Edited, Designed, and Manufactured by Favorite Recipes® Press
P.O. Box 305142
Nashville, Tennessee 37230
1-800-358-0560

Manufactured in the United States of America
First Printing: 1996 10,000 copies

Cover Art
From an original oil painting
by David Conklin,
depicting Bertha Endress Rollo
with her grandfather Keeper Captain Robert Carlson,
commissioned by the Great Lakes Shipwreck Historical Society.

CONTENTS

Acknowledgements

The author wishes to express her sincere appreciation to the following organizations and individuals, whose assistance greatly facilitated the tasks at hand:

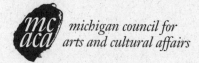

michigan council for arts and cultural affairs

Bertha Endress Rollo

The Great Lakes Shipwreck Historical Society
Board of Directors

Thomas L. Farnquist

Claudia Lewinski

David Conklin

Jeffrey, Cassandra & Jacquline Holt
(official tasters)

Althea Specht

Mitzi Robertson

Andi McDonnell & the great staff at FRP

Contributors

Mary Vogl Barber	Betty A. Holt	Gilbert F. Peterman
Mary Bellinger	Jan M. Holt	Helen Apostle Peterman
Michele Bergeron	Ann Irwin	Jill F. Peterman
Anna Carlson	Elva LaCombe	Mitzi Robertson
Cecelia Carlson Endress	Doris LaPine	Bertha Endress Rollo
Joy S. Harris	Claudia Lewinski	Lynn M. Press
Mary Harris	Roxanne McKiddie	Anna Hattie Vogl

DEDICATION

To Bertha Endress Rollo: your stories have inspired us to do this cookbook and share the culture of this beautiful region.

Bertha Endress Rollo with her grandfather,
Captain Robert Carlson, lightkeeper from
1903 to 1931 at Whitefish Point.

"*We lived our lives in service to the sailors, the travelers on the ships and the shipping companies. That's why my family was at Whitefish Point.*"

Bertha Endress Rollo
Resident, Whitefish Point Lighthouse
1910-1931

HISTORICAL OVERVIEW OF THE WHITEFISH POINT AREA

Chippewa (Ojibwa) Indians were the first inhabitants of the area, literally living off the land and water. Abundant game and fish from surrounding Lake Superior supported the native population. During the 1600s French explorers came to the Whitefish Point area, followed soon after by missionaries and fur traders.

For nearly two hundred years the Chippewas camped at the Point and at the Tahquamenon River mouth in the summers—fishing, hunting, and tanning pelts for trade with the French and British. Gradually commerce increased. In the 1840s the Chippewas established a small commercial fishing village at Whitefish Point. By 1850 quantities of whitefish were being shipped to markets in Chicago and Milwaukee. A series of commercial fisheries has operated from the Point ever since.

Between 1800 and 1850 navigation on Lake Superior also increased with the discovery and mining of copper and iron ore in the Western Upper Peninsula. Whitefish Point was a landmark for navigators seeking the protective shelter of Whitefish Bay and a meeting place for travelers heading east and west. In recognition of the importance of shipping and the treacherous waters around the Point, the first lighthouse on Lake Superior was built at strategic Whitefish Point in 1848 and 1849.

Many ships faltered in the dangerous waters at the eastern end of Lake Superior. In 1876, a lifesaving station was established at Vermilion, some ten miles west of Whitefish Point. Rescue efforts on the part of Vermilion crews saved many sailors' lives. The station operated until 1943.

The vast lowlands and marshes between the Point and Vermilion, gave rise to another chapter of the area's development. Wild cranberries grew in marshes. In the 1870s bogs were cultivated

and cranberries were harvested and shipped from Whitefish Point to Detroit, Buffalo, and Chicago. Cranberry farms were productive here until 1975, when the storm which sank the *Edmund Fitzgerald* altered drainage of the remaining bogs, and subsequent drought caused further damage. Recently, efforts have begun to reintroduce cultivated cranberries near Whitefish Point.

The Paradise–Tahquamenon–Whitefish Point area underwent major change in the 1880s as lumbering interests moved into the region. Logging companies built rails into the forests, cutting and transporting the logs by rail and river to sawmills built at Tahquamenon River mouth at Emerson and at the mouth of the Shelldrake River. Lumber was then shipped to major markets around the Great Lakes. Both Emerson and Shelldrake grew and prospered with the lumber industry into the early 1900s. At one time Shelldrake, three miles north of Paradise, had a seasonal population of more than 1,000. Much of the town was destroyed by fire in 1910, though sawmills continued to operate at declining levels until 1929. Emerson operations shut down in 1913 and the town was abandoned.

The fires which destroyed Shelldrake were common in the lumbered-off area. A widespread fire in 1922 left much of the land barren, but not for long. Natural progression of plants in burned-over areas with sandy, acid soil gives rise to wild blueberries. Fields of "blue gold" grew from the ashes across vast areas. Low-bush varieties that ripen in August and high-bush berries ready in September were picked by as many as 1500 laborers during the height of commercial harvesting, which continued from 1923 to 1934. Berries were supplied to markets in the Midwest. The natural progression of vegetation and forest that produced wild blueberries in abundance also reduced their numbers. Wild blueberries can still be found in quantity in many spots in Whitefish Township.

WHITEFISH POINT LIGHT STATION

Whitefish Point, located in Michigan's northeastern Upper Peninsula, juts into Lake Superior, forming Whitefish Bay to the east; to the west lies two hundred miles of treacherous open water. This extension of land marks the critical turning point for all ships entering or leaving Superior. Since man first began navigating the often turbulent waters of Superior, Whitefish Point was a destination that provided sanctuary from the legendary gales of November that build from the northwest. Here, where the congested up- and down-bound shipping lanes converge, collisions and groundings caused by fog, snow squalls, smoke from forest fires, and human error were not uncommon. These hazards combined have claimed many ships, passengers, and crew. Of the 350 vessels lost on Superior, approximately two-thirds have gone down in the eastern half of the lake, many along an eighty-mile stretch that extends west from Whitefish Point to Munising, Michigan. This deadly coastline has earned the ominous title "Graveyard of the Great Lakes."

Whitefish Point Light Tower and Keeper's Quarters circa 1912.

The first lighthouse on Lake Superior, established at Whitefish Point in 1849, was a direct result of a two-year newspaper campaign by celebrated journalist Horace Greeley. Greeley's efforts raised public awareness for the need of a lifesaving beacon at Whitefish Point. In 1847, the U.S. Government ordered its construction. The original sixty-five-foot stone tower lasted until 1861 when it was replaced by the

present and still-active eighty-foot "iron-pile" tower and keeper's quarters. This new lighthouse, approved by President Lincoln just as the Civil War began, was a strong indication of its importance not only as an aid to navigation but also to the economic security of the region. In the early 1920s, the United States Coast Guard added a surfboat rescue station at Whitefish Point. The efforts of this rescue station saved many lives and vessels from total destruction.

In 1983 the Great Lakes Shipwreck Historical Society took over the Whitefish Point Lighthouse along with several other buildings on the site. In 1985, the Society opened the Great Lakes Shipwreck Museum, in the old chief's quarters, adding a new larger exhibit building in 1987. In 1991, restoration of the 1861 Lightkeepers Quarters was initiated—opening to visitors in 1996.

Restoration of the Keepers Quarters would not have gone nearly as well or accurately if not for the remarkable memory of former lighthouse resident Bertha Endress Rollo. Bertha lived in the lighthouse with her grandfather light keeper Captain Robert Carlson, grandmother, mother, and younger brother from 1910 to 1931. Growing up at this remote light station with few children her own age for companionship, Bertha acquired early in life a strong interest in the natural and human history that unfolded around her. Over the last several years Bertha has worked with the Society writing detailed accounts of life at Whitefish Point. The reflections of life at Whitefish Point found in this book were provided by Bertha, along with some of her family's favorite recipes. We thank her for all her hard work and attention to detail.

Thomas L. Farnquist, Executive Director
The Great Lakes Shipwreck Historical Society

LIFE AT WHITEFISH POINT
With Stories by Bertha Rollo

Growing up on the lonely shores of Lake Superior at Whitefish Point, Michigan, Bertha Endress Rollo usually spent her time without playmates and was incorporated into the adult world at an early age. The lighthouse at Whitefish Point, operated by her grandfather until his retirement from the Lighthouse Service, was her home for most of twenty-one years. Her memories of early experiences of the region combined with historic details make these vignettes a revealing and fascinating trip into the past for the reader. Bertha lived with her grandparents, mother, and a younger brother at the lighthouse from 1920 to 1931, when her grandfather, Captain Robert Carlson, retired after thirty-nine years' service.

A LIGHTHOUSE CHRISTMAS

The Christmas I remember most took place when I was five years old. It was the loveliest Christmas I ever spent at the lighthouse.

In our family it was Grandfather who fussed, making sure we had a good Christmas. The boats ran until almost Christmas Eve and those that ran late all passed the lighthouse covered with ice and with Christmas trees on the pilot houses. Each blew a Christmas salute and Grandfather replied with a foghorn whistle. Some even sent up rockets; it was a happy time.

I went to bed early so Santa Claus would be sure to come. Granddad then went out to the woodshed and brought in a table-top tree he had cut and hidden behind the shed door. Unlike today, you *never* put up the tree until Christmas Eve, and you never took it down until "Little Christmas," or January 6th, which was when the wise men arrived bringing gifts to the baby Jesus.

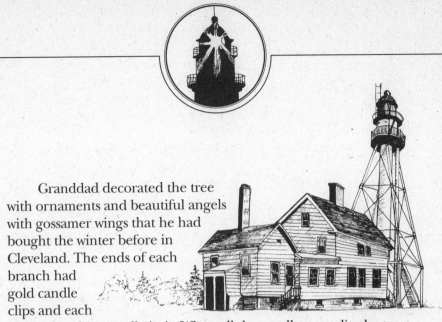

Granddad decorated the tree with ornaments and beautiful angels with gossamer wings that he had bought the winter before in Cleveland. The ends of each branch had gold candle clips and each clip had a white candle in it. When all the candles were lit, the tree was breathtakingly beautiful. My stocking had an orange, apple, a satin (pink, of course, for a girl) bag of fudge, and a green velvet box, which held a little gold ring with a blue stone in it. The stone was Granddad's birthstone, given to me so that I would never forget him.

When we entered the living room, the tree was lit and the phonograph was playing Christmas carols. My gifts were a doll from my mother, with extra clothes she had made (she sewed beautifully), toys from Grandfather and the uncles (my mother's twin brothers), books from my father, long underwear from Grandmother, and other gifts from friends.

Our Christmas dinner was roast chicken, stuffing, mashed potatoes, mashed rutabagas, canned peas, homemade bread, cranberry, and minced pies. This was always Christmas dinner at home; it never varied. And it was good eating, for Grandmother was a good cook. When dinner was over and the dishes were done, we went into the living room and Mother played carols on the organ.

In the evening, Grandmother went to the basement and brought up a big bowl of shiny red apples. Mother passed around plates and knives to everyone except me. They pared the apples and we ate apples until we could eat no more. Granddad read from the Bible the story of Christmas and then we went to bed.

Life at Whitefish Point

The Day Grandmother Panicked

It was the middle of July and ninety-five degrees in the shade. Not a breath of air was stirring and the dog flies were having a field day eating; everything that moved and had blood got bitten. Over on the Lake Superior side the "creosote boys" were repairing the cribs used to prevent erosion.

In the lighthouse kitchen, over a steaming hot stove, Grandmother was getting dinner for the men. She had gotten up at 5:00 a.m. and baked nine loaves of bread, followed by six apple pies. Then she made up cookie dough so that she could make cookies for the boys' evening lunch.

Just as she finished frying a huge platter of venison steak and was ready to put it on the table, she looked out the window and began to sob. Coming in the gate and up the sidewalk was the conservation man for the area. We didn't have beef nor could we get any until the guard boat arrived; we were illegal! The "creosote boys" came in and sat down. Mother put everything on the table but the meat. Granddad came in, looked out the window, and said "Anna, put the meat on the table and set a place for him."

She picked up the platter and with shaking hands brought it to the dining room table and set another place. The Department of Natural Resources man came in and asked Grandmother if she could feed him. She said, "I saw you coming; your place is ready." Grandmother fried another platter of meat and Mother went and got the empty platter.

They had popped the pies in the oven to get warm and, when the plates were removed, the apple pie, cheese, and coffee, along with a platter of cookies, were served. The boys went to their rest house to let their dinner digest and let the heat of the day pass. Their boss said the next meal was to be late—6:30 or 7:00 p.m.

Life at Whitefish Point

D.C.

The last man out of the dining room was the DNR man. He looked Grandmother straight in the eye and gave her a wonderful smile and a big hug. "Mrs. Carlson," he said, "that was the best beefsteak dinner I have ever eaten!"—then went whistling down the sidewalk.

Grandmother sat down and wept with relief.

Life at Whitefish Point

WHERE OUR FOOD CAME FROM

In the spring and fall, the lighthouse tenders brought up supplies that the families had ordered from the Sault. A. H. Eddy and Pete McKinney both had grocery stores and both supplied the lighthouse and Coast Guard with what they needed.

Sears, Roebuck and Montgomery Ward had large food departments and mail ordered all over the country. "Our Own Coffee" came in large cans—red in color and with a bird's nest as the trademark. "Gold-Dust Twins" for cleaning was in everyone's home, as was Fels Naphtha Soap.

The company store and butcher shop at Shelldrake supplied some items, including high-top shoes, which I hated. Our garden supplied potatoes, carrots, string and wax beans, peas, leaf lettuce, radishes, cucumbers, a few cauliflower, horseradish, onions, rutabagas, and cabbage too. Also strawberries.

The woods and water gave us venison (it was unwise to order meat unless by government boat—as the blowflies got it first and spoiled the meat), ducks, geese, partridges, rabbit (snowshoe hare), trout, whitefish, and herring. There was fruit—blueberries, wild strawberries, and cranberries. Sand cherries and beach plums made wonderful jelly.

We had a coffee grinder for our purchased coffee beans and a nutmeg grater for whole nutmegs. Food was very important to my family because we had to feed the men who came to repair the cribs, the submarine signal bell, or anything that Granddad couldn't fix. Besides this, when the Coast Guard men came from Vermillion on a rescue mission, or men from grounded boats or visitors arrived, we fed them all. We also fed peddlers who brought "notions" to the wives such as needles, thread, rickrack and other bindings for aprons,

Life at Whitefish Point

D.C.

bonnets and such, and also
gossip. You couldn't run to the store;
you had to have what you needed on hand.

There was fruit by the bushel—apples,
oranges, lemons—and bananas by the stalk.
"Cotta-suet" by the huge metal pails was used instead
of lard for cakes, cookies, and pies. Bacon grease was saved for meat
frying. Tomatoes and corn came by the big can; it was too cold in the
garden to grow them. Only canned milk was used. Plums, peaches,
and pears we had when they were ripe and we used canned the rest
of the year. Usually, when they were fresh, either Granddad or one of
the fish boats brought them from the Sault.

Life at Whitefish Point

Eating at the Point

Breakfast for the Working Men

The "creosote boys" had the biggest breakfast of all, but then they stood in cold water all morning. Morning, noon, and night, baked beans topped the menu. This was followed by pancakes, bacon or ham, or both, maple syrup (Log Cabin brand), cooked eggs (boiled or fried), stacks of toast, and lots of coffee. Sometimes, for variety, Grandmother served fried potatoes, bacon or ham, baked beans, peas or corn (canned of course), and double-crust pies.

Dinner for the Working Men

In those days dinner was served at noon: Meat, potatoes, the pot of beans, other vegetables, bread and butter, condiments, and two kinds of pie. Cake had been voted down. Cookies, of course, were welcome. And pots of coffee.

Supper for the Working Men

It was repetition of dinner, except the way to prepare the food was different—except for the beans. There was always a "crock of beans." If the potatoes were boiled at noon, they were fried at night. The meat was different: if a roast at noon, then fried ham or such at night. Fish was always at noon. If we had lemon pie at noon, we had apple pie at night. Lemon was the only single-crust pie the workers liked.

On Saturdays, Grandmother's pink pills were the most popular item. With the heavy diet we had to give the workers and no fruit or green stuff (forbidden), you can see why.

Life at Whitefish Point

A Lumberjack Supper

It was in the early nineteen hundreds, when lumbering was big business, that Granddad was invited to take his family and ride the Shelldrake train out to one of their lumber camps. A lumber train of those days was like no other. The roadbed was made of logs and had the look of corduroy. With the underlay, you didn't miss a bump. I was scared stiff and clung tightly to Granddad's shoulders all the way.

While the men were out looking over the area, we went into the camp kitchen to talk to the cook and get warm. The cookstove was a big (and I mean Big) stove. The cook showed Grandmother the huge kettle of boiling potatoes. He then drew a large pan of baked beans from the oven. Next to where the pan of beans had been was a big haunch of venison slowly browning. Next to it, he put a big pan of biscuits. A pot of shelled peas stood ready to be heated. Gravy was in another pan. Onions and beets were sliced and put in vinegar and set on the table. A pot of honey followed. Coffee was the drink served as the men came in from the cold.

The men ate, using their knives as both fork and knife. I was fascinated to see them eat peas with their knives and not drop a single pea. A young lad learning to be a woodsman showed me the secret. He took my knife, dipped it in honey, and then guided my hand into the peas. I ate without losing a single pea! He then proclaimed me a "woodsgirl" as the rest of the men applauded.

Life at Whitefish Point

D.C.

Life at Whitefish Point

Church Services

We had no regular church services to attend. Instead, the area was taken care of by traveling missionaries. When they came, we all gathered at one place (usually the post office) and had a picnic. The minister preached outdoors and then we ate, and then he preached some more.

Grandmother always brought a freezer full of ice cream and a huge bowl of mashed strawberries for topping. I still insist that the ice cream was the best I have ever tasted. The ice cream was hand-churned and I know—for many a time I gladly turned the crank. The ice came from the icehouse and the strawberries from Granddad's garden.

Father Gagnier was the Catholic priest to the Indians and others in the area. One time he came and stayed with us at the lighthouse. What a wonderful man! He told us all kinds of little stories, sang us songs, and told us Indian legends of the area. The Indians loved him and so did we. He walked seventy miles from Sault Ste. Marie to Whitefish Point every month or so, winter or summer.

Life at Whitefish Point

CRANBERRY BOGS OF WHITEFISH

The Village of Whitefish Point started when John Clarke and Alex Barclay spent the winter of 1874 together in a sod hut in the area. Next to a good cave, which there was not, a sod house is the warmest in a land of extreme cold and bitter winds. Alex Barclay sailed as a boat captain during the boat season, but the seasons weren't as long as today by far and the boatmen needed extra money to carry them through the long winters.

Clark and Barclay took Frank House into their plans. They decided to raise cranberries and, in 1875, these three started the first commercial cranberry bog. They homesteaded the area and, using dikes and ditches, they covered the berries with water during periods of frost. From 1890 to 1910, Whitefish Point and Vermillion shipped four to five hundred bushels annually by boat to the big cities.

This cranberry bog of the Frank House family is still in operation and the business now sells their berries to the Ocean Spray Company of Wisconsin.

D.C.

Life at Whitefish Point

SALADS & SOUPS

*...Food was very important to
my family because we had to feed the
men who came to repair the cribs,
the submarine signal bell, or anything
that Granddad couldn't fix.
Besides this, when the Coast Guard
men came from Vermillion on a
rescue mission, or men from
grounded boats or visitors arrived,
we fed them all....*

Whitefish Point Summer Salad

1 cup shredded cold cooked
   whitefish
1 cup diced cold cooked
   potatoes
1/4 cup diced celery
1/2 teaspoon salt
1/4 teaspoon paprika
3/4 cup French dressing

- Combine the whitefish, potatoes and celery in a bowl and toss gently to mix. Add the salt and paprika and mix gently. Add the French dressing, tossing gently to mix.
- Serve on lettuce-lined salad plates. Garnish with strips of pimento.
- Yield: 4 servings.

Lynn M. Press

Chicken and Rice Salad

2 cups chopped cooked chicken
2 cups cooked rice
1 cup chopped celery
1/4 cup chopped green bell
   pepper
1/4 cup chopped green onions
1/4 cup mayonnaise
1 envelop ranch salad
   dressing mix
1/2 teaspoon seasoned salt

- Combine the chicken, rice, celery, green pepper, green onions, mayonnaise, salad dressing mix and seasoned salt in a bowl and mix well.
- Serve in lettuce cups or tomato shells.
- Yield: 6 servings.

Friend of The Shipwreck Society

Salads

Chunky Chicken Salad

8 ounces spiral pasta, cooked
4 chicken breasts, cooked,
  chopped
2 apples, chopped
2 cups white grapes
1 (8-ounce) can pineapple
  chunks
1/2 cup chopped pecans
1 cup cubed Cheddar cheese
1 cup mayonnaise
1 cup sour cream
3 tablespoons lime juice
3 tablespoons honey

- Combine the pasta, chopped chicken, apples, grapes, pineapple, pecans and cheese in a bowl and mix well.
- Combine the mayonnaise, sour cream, lime juice and honey in a bowl and mix well. Add to the chicken salad and toss to mix.
- May substitute almonds for pecans.
- Yield: 8 servings.

Friend of The Shipwreck Society

Tuna Salad

1 (12-ounce) package
  macaroni
1 (9-ounce) can tuna, drained
1 (8-ounce) can green peas,
  drained
1 onion, chopped
1 (2-ounce) jar chopped
  pimento, drained
2 sweet pickles, chopped
3/4 cup mayonnaise
Salt and pepper to taste

- Cook the macaroni using the package directions and drain.
- Combine the macaroni with the tuna, green peas, onion, pimento and pickles in a large bowl and mix well. Add the mayonnaise, salt and pepper. Toss gently to mix.
- Chill in the refrigerator before serving.
- Yield: 6 servings.

Friend of The Shipwreck Society

Salads

Nancy's Winter Salad

Romaine lettuce, torn into
   pieces
Shredded Parmesan cheese
Toasted pecans, coarsely
   chopped
Dried cranberries
Raspberry Vinaigrette Dressing

- Combine the lettuce, cheese, pecans and cranberries in a bowl and toss to mix.
- Add the Raspberry Vinaigrette Dressing and toss until the lettuce is coated. Serve immediately.

Raspberry Vinaigrette Dressing

$1/4$ cup salad oil
$1/3$ cup raspberry vinegar
$1/3$ cup sugar
2 teaspoons salt

- Combine the oil, vinegar, sugar and salt in a bowl and mix well.
- Yield: variable.

Mitzi Robertson

Salads

Fruited Broccoli Salad

1 bunch broccoli, chopped
1 cup raisins
1/2 cup dried cherries
1 apple, chopped
1/2 cup slivered almonds
1 cup shredded white Cheddar
   cheese
1 cup mayonnaise
1/2 cup sugar
1 tablespoon white vinegar

- Combine the broccoli, raisins, cherries, apple, almonds and cheese in a bowl and mix well.
- Combine the mayonnaise, sugar and vinegar in a small bowl and mix well. Add to the salad and toss gently to coat.
- Chill, covered, for 8 to 10 hours before serving.
- Yield: 8 servings.

Friend of The Shipwreck Society

Layered Salad

2 heads lettuce, shredded
Florets of 1 head cauliflower
Florets of 1 bunch broccoli
1 to 2 cups fresh mushrooms,
   sliced
3 or 4 hard-cooked eggs,
   chopped
2 cups shredded Cheddar
   cheese
1 pound bacon, crisp-fried,
   crumbled
1 cup mayonnaise
1 cup sour cream
Garlic salt to taste
Salt and pepper to taste

- Layer the lettuce, cauliflower, broccoli, mushrooms, eggs, cheese and bacon in a large bowl.
- Mix the mayonnaise, sour cream and seasonings in a small bowl. Pour over the layered salad.
- Yield: 20 to 25 servings.

Friend of The Shipwreck Society

Salads

Potluck Potato Salad

10 potatoes, boiled
1 head cabbage, shredded
Salt and pepper to taste
Celery seeds to taste
3 onions, sliced into rings
3 green bell peppers, sliced
  into rings
6 carrots, shredded
6 hard-cooked eggs, sliced
1 cup (or more) mayonnaise
Paprika to taste

- Peel and slice the potatoes. Layer $1/2$ of the cabbage and potatoes in a large bowl. Sprinkle with salt, pepper and celery seeds. Add layers of $1/2$ of the onions, green peppers, carrots and eggs. Spread $1/2$ of the mayonnaise over the eggs.
- Repeat the layers, ending with the mayonnaise. Sprinkle with paprika.
- Chill, covered, for 25 hours or longer.
- Yield: 10 servings.

Friend of The Shipwreck Society

Cranberry Waldorf Salad

2 cups fresh cranberries,
  ground
$1/3$ cup honey
2 cups chopped, unpeeled tart
  apples
1 cup seedless green grape
  halves
$1/2$ cup chopped English
  walnuts
$1/4$ teaspoon salt
1 cup whipping cream,
  whipped

- Combine the cranberries with the honey in a bowl and mix well. Chill, covered, for 8 to 10 hours.
- Add the apples, grapes, walnuts and salt to the cranberries and mix well. Fold the whipped cream into the salad. Spoon into a salad bowl. Chill for several hours.
- Garnish with green grape clusters and whole fresh cranberries.
- Yield: 8 servings.

Friend of The Shipwreck Society

Salads

Frozen Cranberry Banana Salad

1 (20-ounce) can pineapple
  tidbits
5 medium firm bananas
1 (16-ounce) can whole
  cranberry sauce
½ cup sugar
12 ounces whipped topping
½ cup chopped walnuts

- Drain the pineapple juice into a medium bowl and reserve the pineapple.
- Cut the bananas into halves lengthwise. Cut into slices. Add the bananas to the pineapple juice, stirring gently to coat.
- Combine the cranberry sauce and sugar in a large bowl and mix well. Remove the bananas from the pineapple juice and add to the cranberry sauce, discarding the juice. Add the reserved pineapple, whipped topping and walnuts. Toss gently to mix. Pour into a 9x13-inch dish. Freeze until firm.
- Remove the salad from the freezer 15 minutes before serving. Cut into squares.
- Yield: 12 to 16 servings.

Jan Holt

Salads

Gleeson's

1 cup water
2 tablespoons vegetable oil
1 teaspoon salt
1 egg
2½ to 2¾ cups flour
2 to 3 quarts chicken broth

- Combine the water, oil, salt and egg in a large bowl and mix well.
- Reserve ¼ cup of the flour. Add the remaining flour to the mixture and blend well.
- Place the dough on a lightly floured surface. Knead in the reserved ¼ cup flour until the dough is stiff. Roll out the dough until very thin. Cut into 2-inch squares.
- Bring the chicken broth to a boil in a large saucepan. Drop the dough squares into the boiling broth. Simmer for 30 minutes, stirring occasionally.
- May substitute beef broth for the chicken broth.
- Yield: variable.

Betty A. Holt

Soups

Chili

1 pound ground beef
8 ounces ground lean pork
2 tablespoons vegetable oil
1¹/₂ cups chopped onions
1 cup chopped celery
1 small clove of garlic, finely
    chopped
¹/₂ green bell pepper, chopped
2 cups canned tomatoes
1 to 2 tablespoons chili powder
2 tablespoons cold water
2 teaspoons salt
1 teaspoon sugar
1 teaspoon Worcestershire
    sauce
4 cups drained canned kidney
    beans

- Brown the ground beef and pork in the oil in a skillet, stirring until crumbly; drain. Add the onions, celery, garlic and green pepper. Cook for 10 minutes or until the onions are golden brown, stirring frequently.
- Add the tomatoes, chili powder, cold water, salt, sugar and Worcestershire sauce. Bring to a boil over medium heat, stirring occasionally. Simmer, covered, over low heat for 1 hour, stirring occasionally.
- Add the beans. Cook, uncovered, until of the desired thickness, stirring occasionally.
- Yield: 6 servings.

Lynn M. Press

Soups

Upper Peninsula Venison Chili

2 to 4 pounds ground venison
1 cup chopped onions
1/4 cup vegetable oil
3 cups canned tomatoes,
    chopped
2 teaspoons salt
2 tablespoons chili powder
8 cups canned kidney beans
2 to 3 bay leaves

- Sauté the venison and onions in the oil in a skillet, stirring until crumbly. Drain the mixture.
- Add the tomatoes, salt, chili powder, kidney beans and bay leaves. Simmer, covered, over low heat for 1 hour, stirring occasionally. Remove the bay leaves.
- Yield: variable.

Friend of The Shipwreck Society

Finnish Fish Soup

1 large fish
5 potatoes, peeled, chopped
1 onion, chopped
Salt and pepper to taste
1/4 cup butter
2 cups milk

- Cut the fish into chunks. Combine the fish with just enough water to cover in a saucepan. Simmer until the fish flakes easily and drain.
- Combine the potatoes, onion, salt and pepper in just enough water to cover in a saucepan. Simmer until the potatoes are tender, stirring occasionally. Add the fish, butter and milk. Simmer for 30 minutes, stirring occasionally.
- Yield: 6 servings.

Roxanne McKiddie

Soups

Clear Fish Soup with Trout

2 to 4 pounds lake trout
1 to 2 quarts water
1 tablespoon to 1½
   tablespoons whole
   peppercorns
1 teaspoon to 1 tablespoon
   whole allspice
1 medium onion, finely
   chopped
1 carrot, finely chopped
Salt to taste

- Wrap the trout in cheesecloth and tie securely.
- Combine the water, peppercorns, allspice, onion, carrot and salt in a large stockpot. Bring to a boil. Add the trout. Simmer until the trout flakes easily, stirring occasionally. Remove the trout to a platter. Remove the cheesecloth and discard.
- Serve the trout hot or cold, garnished with mayonnaise, lemon slices or tartar sauce.
- Serve the broth, strained or unstrained, in small soup cups.
- May add a few whole cloves to the broth before cooking.
- Yield: variable.

Anna M. Carlson

Fish Chowder

1 pound skinless boneless
  whitefish
2 (10-ounce) cans chopped
  clams
1 large onion, chopped
1 clove of garlic, minced
3 carrots, chopped
3 ribs celery with leaves,
  chopped
2 large potatoes, chopped
Lemon pepper to taste
1 cup light cream
1 cup (or more) milk

- Combine the whitefish, undrained clams, onion, garlic, carrots, celery, potatoes and lemon pepper in a saucepan. Add enough water to cover the mixture. Simmer, covered, for 20 to 25 minutes or until the potatoes are tender, stirring occasionally. Remove from the heat.
- Stir in the light cream and milk, adding additional milk if needed to cover. Heat just to the boiling point, stirring occasionally.
- Ladle into soup bowls. Garnish with pats of butter and ground pepper.
- Yield: 6 servings.

Christel Goese

Soups

Hamburger Soup

1½ pounds ground beef
2 teaspoons vegetable oil
1½ quarts water
2 cups chopped potatoes
1 cup chopped celery
¼ cup uncooked rice
1 cup chopped carrots
½ cup chopped onion
2 cups chopped tomatoes
1 cup chopped rutabaga
1 tablespoon salt

- Brown the ground beef in the oil in a skillet, stirring until crumbly; drain.
- Combine the ground beef, water, potatoes, celery, rice, carrots, onion, tomatoes, rutabagas and salt in a stockpot. Bring to a boil over medium heat, stirring occasionally. Simmer over low heat for 1 hour, stirring occasionally.
- Yield: 6 servings.

Friend of The Shipwreck Society

Venison Soup

2 to 4 pounds ground venison
6 to 7 carrots, sliced
2 onions, chopped
½ rutabaga, finely chopped
2 to 3 potatoes, cubed
1 (16-ounce) can tomatoes,
    mashed
½ small head cabbage,
    chopped
1½ to 2 quarts water
1 tablespoon salt
1 tablespoon pepper
Celery salt to taste
1 bay leaf

- Combine the venison and next 7 ingredients in a stockpot. Add the salt, pepper, celery salt and bay leaf.
- Bring to a boil over medium heat, stirring occasionally. Simmer over low heat until the vegetables are tender, stirring occasionally. Degrease the soup if necessary and remove the bay leaf.
- Note: Grandmother would put an ice cube in a piece of cheesecloth and swish it around the top of the soup to remove the grease.
- Yield: 6 to 8 servings.

Anna Carlson

Soups

Bean Soup

2 cups dried white beans
8 cups boiling water
2 to 3 ham hocks or ham bone
1 envelope dry onion soup mix
1/2 cup catsup
1 teaspoon salt
1/2 teaspoon savory
1 large carrot, finely chopped
Pepper to taste
3 ribs celery, finely chopped

- Rinse and sort the beans. Place in a large saucepan. Add the boiling water. Simmer, covered, until the beans are plump, stirring occasionally.
- Add the ham hocks, soup mix, catsup, salt, savory, carrot and pepper. Simmer until the beans are almost tender. Add the celery and up to 5 additional cups boiling water. Simmer until the celery is tender, stirring occasionally.
- Yield: 6 to 8 servings.

Friend of The Shipwreck Society

Cabbage and Barley Soup

1/2 cup barley
2 cups water
1 small cabbage, chopped
1 medium carrot, chopped
1/2 small onion, finely chopped
1 cup chopped cooked roast
  beef
1 tablespoon salt
Dash of pepper

- Cook the barley in a large saucepan until soft using the package directions. Add the water, cabbage, carrot, onion, roast beef, salt and pepper.
- Simmer over low heat until the cabbage is tender, stirring occasionally.
- May add additional water for thinner soup.
- Yield: 4 servings.

Friend of The Shipwreck Society

Soups

Corn Chowder

1 cup chopped potatoes
1 cup boiling water
3 slices bacon, chopped
1 medium onion, chopped
1½ cups canned whole kernel
   corn
1 cup milk
Salt and pepper to taste
2 tablespoons chopped parsley

- Combine the potatoes and boiling water in a saucepan. Cook, covered, for 10 to 15 minutes, stirring occasionally.
- Fry the bacon in a skillet until some of the fat is rendered. Add the onion. Sauté until the onion is soft and the bacon is brown. Drain the mixture.
- Add the bacon mixture and corn to the potatoes. Simmer over low heat until the potatoes are tender, stirring occasionally. Add the milk, salt and pepper. Heat just to serving temperature.
- Spoon into serving bowls. Top with the parsley.
- Yield: 4 servings.

Friend of The Shipwreck Society

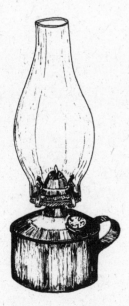

Soups

Old-Fashioned Split Pea Soup

1 cup dried split peas
6 cups boiling water
1 ham bone or pieces of cubed
   ham
1 carrot, grated
2 medium onions, minced
1 potato, grated
¼ cup finely chopped celery
¼ cup finely chopped green
   bell pepper
Salt and pepper to taste

- Combine the split peas and boiling water in a large saucepan. Let stand for 1 hour.
- Add the ham bone, carrot, onions, potato, celery, green pepper, salt and pepper to the peas. Simmer over low heat until the peas are tender, stirring occasionally.
- Add additional water if needed for soup consistency. Simmer for 5 to 10 minutes longer.
- Yield: 4 servings.

Friend of The Shipwreck Society

Ham Sandwich

Grandmother grew tired of plain ham sandwiches one day and took out the meat grinder and went to work. I was eating sweet pickles at the time so she took some of those and ground them up too. She tasted the ham and pickles and added some chopped onion. Then she took some of the mayonnaise that Mother had made and added some of that. Thus Grandmother's ham sandwiches were born.

German Potato Soup

8 ounces bacon, chopped
1 onion, chopped
1 cup chopped celery
2 large potatoes, finely chopped
Salt and pepper to taste
1 (5-ounce) can evaporated
   milk
1 (10-ounce) can cream of
   mushroom soup
Dash of Worcestershire sauce
Garlic powder to taste

- Sauté the bacon with the onion in a saucepan until crisp and drain.
- Add the celery, potatoes, salt and pepper to the saucepan. Add enough water to cover. Simmer over low heat until the vegetables are tender, stirring occasionally.
- Add the evaporated milk, soup, Worcestershire sauce and garlic powder. Heat just to serving temperature. Purée in a blender or crush with a potato masher.
- Yield: 4 servings.

Friend of The Shipwreck Society

Tomato Soup

1/4 cup rice
1 cup water
1 (16-ounce) can whole
   tomatoes
1/2 small onion, finely chopped
1 cup chopped cooked roast
   beef
1 tablespoon salt
Dash of pepper

- Cook the rice in the water in a saucepan until tender. Add the undrained tomatoes, onion, beef, salt and pepper.
- Simmer over low heat for 1 hour, stirring occasionally.
- Yield: 2 servings.

Friend of The Shipwreck Society

Soups

Vegetables
& Side Dishes

...The men ate, using their
knives as both fork and knife.
I was fascinated to see them eat peas
with their knives and not drop a
single pea. A young lad learning to be
a woodsman showed me the secret.
He took my knife, dipped it
in honey, and then guided my hand
into the peas. I ate without losing
a single pea!...

Sunday-Best Baked Macaroni and Cheese

8 to 9 ounces elbow macaroni
3 tablespoons butter
3 tablespoons flour
3 cups milk
1 teaspoon salt
1/4 teaspoon pepper
3/4 cup shredded sharp
   Cheddar cheese
1 tablespoon chopped onion
1/2 teaspoon dry mustard
1/2 to 1 teaspoon
   Worcestershire sauce
Bread crumbs

- Cook the macaroni using the package directions.
- Melt the butter in a saucepan. Combine the flour and 1 cup of the milk in a jar with a tightfitting lid and shake until well mixed. Pour into the melted butter. Stir in the remaining 2 cups milk, salt and pepper.
- Cook until thickened, stirring constantly. Add the cheese, onion, dry mustard and Worcestershire sauce. Heat until the cheese is melted, stirring frequently.
- Alternate layers of macaroni and cheese sauce in a greased casserole until all ingredients are used. Sprinkle bread crumbs on top.
- Bake at 350 degrees for 25 minutes.
- Yield: 6 servings.

Roxanne McKiddie

Vegetables & Side Dishes

Grandmother's Poultry Bread Stuffing

10 to 12 cups dried bread
   cubes
1 medium onion, chopped
Salt and pepper to taste
Sage and poultry seasoning to
   taste
2 to 3 tablespoons bacon
   drippings

- Combine the bread cubes, onion, salt, pepper, sage, poultry seasoning and bacon drippings in a bowl and mix well.
- Use to stuff chickens and other birds except ducks. For ducks substitute orange juice for the bacon drippings to moisten the stuffing.
- Yield: variable.

Anna Carlson

Calico Beans

1 pound ground beef
1 medium onion, chopped
1 pound bacon
1/2 cup sugar
1/2 cup packed brown sugar
1/2 cup catsup
1 (16-ounce) can Great
   Northern beans
1 (16-ounce) can kidney beans
1 (16-ounce) can pork and
   beans
1 (16-ounce) can butter beans

- Brown the ground beef with the onion in a skillet, stirring until crumbly; drain.
- Brown the bacon in a skillet until crisp. Drain and crumble.
- Combine the ground beef, bacon, sugar, brown sugar and catsup in a large bowl and mix well.
- Add the beans and mix well. Spoon into a greased baking dish.
- Bake at 325 degrees for 1 1/2 hours.
- Yield: 12 servings.

Lynn M. Press

Vegetables & Side Dishes

Snappers

2 pounds (4 cups) dried navy
    beans
1 to 1¹/₂ teaspoons salt
3 to 4 tablespoons brown sugar
2 teaspoons dry mustard
1 onion, chopped
¹/₄ to ¹/₃ cup molasses
1 teaspoon ground ginger
8 ounces salt pork or bacon

- Combine the beans with enough water to cover in a large saucepan. Let stand for 8 to 10 hours and drain.
- Add enough cold water to cover. Bring to a boil over medium heat. Simmer over low heat until the skins pop, stirring occasionally. Drain the beans.
- Add the salt, brown sugar, dry mustard, onion, molasses and ginger to the beans and mix well. Pour into a large baking dish or bean pot.
- Add enough hot water to cover.
- Place enough water to cover the salt pork in a saucepan. Bring to a boil. Place the salt pork in the water for 1 minute. Remove and cut deep slits 1 inch apart in the rind.
- Place the salt pork in the beans, leaving only the rind exposed.
- Bake, covered, in a slow oven until the beans are tender, adding additional water when needed to keep the beans covered. Remove the cover. Bake for 30 minutes longer.
- Yield: 8 to 10 servings.

Anna Carlson

Vegetables & Side Dishes

Carrot Loaf

2 bunches carrots, cooked,
   mashed
2 cups cornflakes, finely
   crushed
1 egg, beaten
1 tablespoon melted butter or
   margarine
2 teaspoons finely chopped
   onion
1 teaspoon parsley flakes
1 teaspoon salt
$1/8$ teaspoon nutmeg
$1/2$ cup thick white sauce

- Combine the carrots, cornflakes, egg, butter, onion, parsley flakes, salt, nutmeg and white sauce in a bowl and mix well. Pour into a greased loaf pan.
- Bake at 350 degrees for 50 minutes.
- Yield: 10 servings.

Friend of The Shipwreck Society

Corn Pudding

3 cups fresh corn
$1^1/2$ teaspoons salt
$1/4$ teaspoon pepper
2 tablespoons melted butter
3 eggs, beaten
1 cup milk

- Combine the corn, salt, pepper, butter, eggs and milk in a bowl and mix well. Pour into a buttered casserole. Garnish with pimento or green pepper. Place the casserole in a shallow baking pan. Add water to $1/2$-inch depth.
- Bake at 350 degrees for 1 to $1^1/2$ hours.
- Yield: 6 servings.

Friend of The Shipwreck Society

Vegetables & Side Dishes

Mashed Potato Casserole

6³/₄ cups water
9 tablespoons margarine
1 teaspoon salt
2¹/₂ teaspoons onion salt
7 cups dry instant mashed
    potatoes
2 cups sour cream
8 ounces cream cheese, softened
2¹/₄ cups milk
Shredded cheese

- Combine the water, margarine, salt and onion salt in a saucepan. Bring to a boil, stirring occasionally.
- Combine the water mixture and instant potatoes in a mixer bowl and beat well. Add the sour cream, cream cheese and milk and beat well. Pour into a greased casserole. Sprinkle cheese over the top.
- Bake at 350 degrees until bubbly.
- Yield: 12 servings.

Friend of The Shipwreck Society

Horseradish Delight Sandwich

(The only ones delighted with these were Granddad and me.) Granddad brought horseradish roots with him, and those plants, along with plants that Keeper Kimball had left, formed a nice small bed of roots. Every fall, Granddad and I took a small shovel and, after dark, went to the horseradish bed and dug up roots. Then we washed the dirt off at the yard pump and went in the kitchen to start our ritual.

Granddad sent me to the basement for big round Bermuda onions. They were good and juicy and sweet in those days. Granddad sliced a loaf of Grandmother's bread, buttered it, put on some of Mother's salad dressing, put on the horseradish he had grated (and I had to watch him), and then the sliced onions. He combined them all into big, thick sandwiches, and with tears running down our faces we ate them. "Gosh, but it is good," I said.

Vegetables & Side Dishes

Shelldrake Stuffed Baked Potatoes

4 medium potatoes
1/4 cup milk
1/8 teaspoon pepper
1/4 cup butter, softened
1 teaspoon salt
1/4 cup crumbled crisp-cooked
   bacon
1/4 cup shredded Cheddar
   cheese
1/4 cup finely chopped green
   onions
Paprika

- Place the potatoes in a baking pan. Bake at 425 degrees for 50 minutes or until soft.
- Cut a thin slice from the top of each potato and discard. Scoop out the potato pulp, reserving the potato skins. Combine the potato pulp, milk, pepper, butter and salt in a bowl and mix well. Spoon the mixture into the reserved potato skins. Sprinkle the bacon, cheese and green onions on top. Sprinkle with paprika. Wrap in plastic wrap. Chill for 8 to 10 hours.
- Remove the plastic wrap and place the potatoes in a baking pan.
- Bake at 425 degrees for 30 to 40 minutes or until the potatoes are heated through and the tops are golden brown.
- Yield: 4 servings.

Friend of The Shipwreck Society

Vegetables & Side Dishes

Potato Curry (Fried Potatoes)

4 large potatoes, peeled
1/4 teaspoon mustard seeds
5 tablespoons vegetable oil
6 tablespoons chopped onion
3/4 teaspoon salt
1/2 teaspoon red chili powder
  or red pepper

- Cut the potatoes into 1/2-inch chunks.
- Sauté the mustard seeds in the hot oil in a large skillet until the seeds crack. Add the onion. Fry until golden brown. Add the potatoes, salt and chili powder. Stir-fry over low heat until the potatoes are tender and golden brown. Serve hot.
- Yield: 6 servings.

Friend of The Shipwreck Society

Potatoes Royale

1 (24-ounce) package frozen
  hash brown potatoes
1 (10-ounce) can cream of
  chicken soup
6 to 8 ounces shredded sharp
  Cheddar cheese
1 cup sour cream
1/2 cup chopped onion
1 teaspoon salt
Dash of pepper
1/2 cup melted butter

- Thaw the potatoes enough to separate.
- Combine the potatoes, soup, cheese, sour cream, onion, salt, pepper and butter in a large bowl and toss gently to mix. Pour into a greased 9x13-inch baking dish.
- Bake at 325 degrees for 40 to 50 minutes or until golden brown.
- Yield: 6 servings.

Friend of The Shipwreck Society

Vegetables & Side Dishes

Cranberry Squash

1 egg, beaten
2 tablespoons melted butter
3 cups mashed cooked squash
3/4 cup cranberries
1/4 cup frozen orange juice
   concentrate
2 tablespoons honey
Pinch of nutmeg
1/2 cup chopped walnuts
2 tablespoons melted butter

- Combine the egg, 2 tablespoons butter and squash in a bowl and mix well.
- Combine the cranberries, orange juice concentrate, honey and nutmeg in a bowl and mix well.
- Add 1/4 cup of the cranberry mixture to the squash mixture and mix well. Spoon into a buttered casserole. Top with the remaining cranberry mixture. Sprinkle with the walnuts and drizzle with the remaining 2 tablespoons butter.
- Bake at 400 degrees for 25 minutes.
- Yield: 6 servings.

Mitzi Robertson

Home First Aid

 Cloves—Toothache.
Onions—Poultice for chest, sliced onions and sugar for cough syrup.

Vegetables & Side Dishes

Summer Squash Italiano

2 carrots, thinly sliced
1 onion, chopped
1 clove of garlic, minced
2 tablespoons vegetable oil
1 pound zucchini, sliced
1 pound yellow crookneck
   squash, sliced
2 tomatoes, chopped
2 tablespoons vinegar
1 teaspoon salt
1/4 teaspoon basil
1/4 teaspoon chili powder
Dash of pepper

- Combine the carrots, onion and garlic in the oil in a large skillet. Cook, covered, for 5 minutes, stirring occasionally. Add the zucchini, squash, tomatoes, vinegar, salt, basil, chili powder and pepper. Cook, covered, over medium heat for 10 minutes or until the vegetables are tender, stirring occasionally.
- Yield: 8 servings.

Friend of The Shipwreck Society

Vegetables & Side Dishes

Zucchini Casserole

2 pounds zucchini
2 pounds (4 medium)
  tomatoes, peeled
1 teaspoon oregano
2 teaspoons salt
1/2 teaspoon pepper
1/2 teaspoon garlic powder
1/2 cup dried minced onion
2 tablespoons vegetable oil

- Cut the zucchini and the tomatoes into 1/2-inch slices.
- Combine the oregano, salt, pepper and garlic powder in a bowl and mix well.
- Layer 1/2 of the zucchini and 1/2 of the tomatoes in a 6x10-inch baking dish, sprinkling with all the minced onion and 1/2 of the seasoning mixture. Layer the remaining zucchini and 1/4 of the remaining seasoning over the onion.
- Bake, covered, at 375 degrees for 30 minutes. Remove the cover.
- Arrange the remaining tomatoes on top. Brush with the vegetable oil and sprinkle with the remaining seasoning.
- Bake, uncovered, for 30 minutes longer.
- Yield: 12 servings.

Friend of The Shipwreck Society

Vegetables & Side Dishes

Cranberry Conserve

4 cups cranberries, cut into
   halves
1 tablespoon grated orange
   peel
2 oranges, peeled, sliced and
   cut into quarters
1¼ cups water
1 cup raisins
2½ cups sugar
1 cup chopped pecans

- Combine the cranberries, orange peel, oranges, water and raisins in a large saucepan. Simmer over low heat until the cranberries are soft, stirring occasionally. Add the sugar and pecans. Simmer for 10 to 15 minutes longer, stirring frequently.
- Spoon into storage containers. Seal and store in the refrigerator.
- Yield: 3 pints.

Mitzi Robertson

D.C.

Vegetables & Side Dishes

Cran-Raspberry Jam

2 (10-ounce) packages frozen
    sweetened raspberries,
    thawed
4 cups fresh or frozen
    cranberries
5 cups sugar
1 (1³/₄-ounce) envelope
    powdered fruit pectin

- Drain the raspberries, reserving the juice. Add enough water to the raspberry juice to measure 1¹/₂ cups.
- Combine the raspberry juice, raspberries, cranberries and sugar in a large saucepan. Bring to a full rolling boil, stirring occasionally. Boil for 1 minute, stirring constantly. Remove from the heat.
- Skim off the foam. Pour into hot sterilized jars, leaving ¹/₄ inch headspace. Seal with 2-piece lids. Place in a boiling water bath for 15 minutes.
- Yield: six ¹/₂ pints.

Joy S. Harris

Vegetables & Side Dishes

Main Dishes

*...The last man out of the
dining room was the DNR man.
He looked Grandmother straight
in the eye and gave her a wonderful
smile and a big hug. "Mrs. Carlson,"
he said, "that was the best
beefsteak dinner I have ever eaten!"–
then went whistling down
the sidewalk.
Grandmother sat down and
wept with relief....*

Jugged Beaver

1 onion, chopped
1 cup red wine
1 beaver
5 slices bacon
Flour seasoned with salt and
   pepper
1 clove of garlic, chopped
1 bay leaf
¼ teaspoon thyme
1 cup water

- Combine the onion and wine in a shallow dish and mix well. Add the beaver, turning to coat both sides. Marinate, covered, in the refrigerator for 8 to 10 hours, turning occasionally. Drain the beaver and reserve the marinade.
- Fry the bacon in a heavy skillet until crisp. Remove the bacon, reserving the bacon drippings.
- Coat the beaver with the seasoned flour. Add to the bacon drippings in the skillet. Fry over medium heat until brown on both sides.
- Crumble the bacon. Add the bacon, garlic, bay leaf, thyme, reserved marinade and 1 cup water to the skillet. Simmer, covered, over very low heat for 2½ hours.
- Remove the beaver to a hot platter and keep warm. Remove the bay leaf. May add flour to the pan drippings to make gravy.
- Yield: variable.

Friend of The Shipwreck Society

Main Dishes

Beef Jerky

Beef or venison
Liquid smoke
Seasoned salt
Garlic salt
Pepper

- Cut the beef or venison with the grain into strips.
- Layer the strips in a dish, sprinkling each layer with the liquid smoke, seasoned salt, garlic salt and pepper. Marinate, covered, in the refrigerator for 8 to 10 hours.
- Place the strips close together but not overlapping on a rack in a baking pan. Place in the oven with the oven light on. Let stand for about 8 hours.
- Yield: variable.

Friend of The Shipwreck Society

Main Dishes

Oven Beef

2 pounds boneless stew beef
   chunks
6 carrots, cut into chunks
1 rib celery, cut into chunks
3 onions, cut into chunks
6 potatoes, cut into chunks
2 tablespoons tapioca
1 tablespoon sugar
2 teaspoons salt
2 teaspoons pepper
1 cup tomato juice

- Arrange the beef in a greased casserole. Add the vegetables.
- Mix the tapioca, sugar, salt and pepper in a bowl. Sprinkle over the vegetables and beef. Pour in the tomato juice.
- Bake, covered, at 250 degrees for 4 hours.
- Yield: 8 servings.

Doris LaPine

Dried Beef Casserole

1/4 cup chopped onion
1/4 cup chopped celery
4 ounces dried chipped beef,
   shredded
1/4 cup butter or margarine
1/4 cup flour
1 cup (or more) milk
2 cups macaroni, cooked
1/4 teaspoon pepper
1/2 teaspoon salt
1 teaspoon dried parsley
1/3 cup shredded American
   cheese

- Sauté the onion, celery and beef in the butter in a skillet until the onion is soft but not brown. Stir in the flour until well mixed. Add the milk gradually.
- Cook until the sauce is thickened, stirring constantly. Stir in the macaroni, pepper, salt and parsley. Spoon into a greased 1 1/2-quart casserole. Sprinkle with the cheese.
- Bake at 350 degrees for 15 minutes.
- Yield: 6 servings.

Marie Tunnell

Main Dishes

Aunt Mary's Meatballs and Sauce

1½ *pounds spareribs*
1 *(8-ounce) can tomato paste*
1 *(15-ounce) can tomato sauce*
1½ *tomato sauce cans water*
Oregano to taste
Parsley to taste
Meatballs

- Brown the spareribs in a large nonstick skillet over medium heat. Add the tomato paste, tomato sauce, water, oregano and parsley. Add the Meatballs.
- Simmer, covered, over low heat for 2½ hours, stirring occasionally. Remove the cover. Simmer for 30 minutes longer or until thickened, stirring occasionally.

Meatballs

2 *pounds ground beef*
¾ *cup bread crumbs*
¾ *cup grated Romano cheese*
2 *eggs*
1 *clove of garlic, finely chopped*
¼ *cup chopped parsley*
Oregano to taste
Salt and pepper to taste

- Combine the ground beef, bread crumbs, cheese, eggs, garlic, parsley, oregano, salt and pepper in a bowl and mix well. Shape into meatballs.
- Yield: 8 servings.

Mary Bellinger

Cabbage and Ground Beef Casserole

3 cups shredded cabbage
¾ cup cooked rice
1 pound ground beef
1 (6-ounce) can tomato paste
1 (10-ounce) can tomato soup
2 cups water
1 medium onion, chopped
1 teaspoon salt
1 teaspoon sugar
¼ teaspoon pepper
¼ teaspoon garlic powder
¼ teaspoon marjoram

- Layer the cabbage, rice and uncooked ground beef in a greased 2-quart casserole.
- Combine the tomato paste, soup, water, onion, salt, sugar, pepper, garlic powder and marjoram in a saucepan. Bring to a boil over medium heat, stirring occasionally. Pour over the layers.
- Bake, uncovered, at 350 degrees for 1 hour.
- Yield: 8 servings.

Friend of The Shipwreck Society

Home First Aid

 Castor Oil—To shine patent leather shoes.
Black Tea—To settle upset stomach, to dye white stockings tan.

Main Dishes

Greek Casserole (Mousaka Kreas)

¹/₂ clove of garlic, sliced
2 tablespoons vegetable oil
1 bay leaf, crumbled
1 teaspoon ground sage
1 teaspoon salt
Pepper to taste
1 pound ground beef
¹/₂ clove of garlic, sliced
6 cups thinly sliced potatoes
1 cup sliced onions
2 teaspoons salt
1 (16-ounce) can tomatoes
Paprika to taste

- Sauté ¹/₂ clove of garlic in the oil in a large skillet. Remove the garlic and discard. Add the bay leaf, sage, 1 teaspoon salt, pepper and ground beef. Brown the ground beef, stirring until crumbly. Remove the ground beef to a bowl.
- Sauté the remaining ¹/₂ clove of garlic. Remove the garlic and discard. Add the potatoes. Cook until brown, stirring frequently. Add the onions and 2 teaspoons salt, mixing well.
- Layer the ground beef, potato mixture and tomatoes in a 2¹/₂-quart casserole ¹/₃ at a time in the order given.
- Bake, covered, at 375 degrees for 1 hour or until the vegetables are tender. Sprinkle with paprika just before serving.
- Yield: 12 servings.

Helen Apostle Peterman

Main Dishes

Swedish Meatballs

2 pounds ground chuck
2/3 cup bread crumbs
1 (10-ounce) can beef
*   consommé*
4 teaspoons minced onion
2 teaspoons salt
1/4 teaspoon pepper
Vegetable oil for frying
Flour
1 (10-ounce) can cream of
*   mushroom soup*
1 soup can water

- Combine the ground chuck, bread crumbs, consommé, onion, salt and pepper in a bowl and mix well.
- Let stand, covered, in the refrigerator for 30 minutes or longer. Shape into meatballs.
- Fry the meatballs in hot oil in a large skillet, turning to brown all sides. Place in a baking dish, reserving the pan drippings.
- Bake at 200 degrees for 30 minutes.
- Blend flour into the pan drippings, stirring until well mixed. Add the mushroom soup and water, mixing well. Bring to a boil, stirring frequently. Pour over the meatballs. Garnish with parsley.
- May substitute red wine for the mushroom soup.
- Yield: 8 servings.

Friend of The Shipwreck Society

Main Dishes

Beef and Potato Loaf

1 pound ground beef
3/4 cup evaporated milk
1/2 cup fine cracker crumbs
1/4 cup catsup
1/4 onion, sliced
1 teaspoon salt
1/4 teaspoon pepper
4 cups sliced potatoes
1 tablespoon chopped onion
1 teaspoon salt
1/4 teaspoon pepper

- Combine the ground beef, evaporated milk, cracker crumbs, catsup, sliced onion, 1 teaspoon salt and 1/4 teaspoon pepper in a bowl and mix well.
- Layer the potatoes, chopped onion and remaining 1 teaspoon salt and 1/4 teaspoon pepper in a greased 2-quart casserole. Spread the ground beef mixture over the potatoes.
- Bake at 350 degrees for 1 hour or until the potatoes are tender and the beef is brown.
- Yield: 6 servings.

Friend of The Shipwreck Society

Main Dishes

Upper Peninsula Pasties

4 cups flour
2 teaspoons salt
1½ cups shortening
10 tablespoons ice water
1 pound lean beef, cut into
  cubes
1 pound coarsely ground lean
  beef
1 pound lean pork, cut into
  small cubes
5 large potatoes, peeled,
  chopped
1½ cups small rutabaga cubes
2 large onions, chopped
1 tablespoon salt
1 teaspoon fresh ground
  pepper

• Mix the flour and salt in a large chilled bowl. Cut in the shortening with a pastry blender until the mixture is crumbly. Add the ice water all at once; mix well, adding additional water if needed to hold the dough together. Divide the dough into 6 portions.

• Combine the beef cubes, ground beef, pork, potatoes, rutabaga, onions, salt and pepper in a bowl and mix well.

• Roll each portion of dough into a ¼-inch thick circle on a lightly floured surface. Place 1½ cups beef mixture in the center of each dough circle. Fold up sides of dough to enclose the filling, overlapping the edges and pressing together to seal. Crimp the edge and cut a vent. Place on a baking sheet.

• Bake at 400 degrees for 45 to 50 minutes or until golden brown. Serve with catsup and dill pickles.

• Yield: 6 servings.

Claudia Lewinski

Main Dishes

Gumpkies (Stuffed Cabbage)

3 medium firm heads cabbage
2 pounds ground lean pork
2 pounds ground veal
1 pound ground beef
2 onions, grated
2 teaspoons parsley flakes
2 carrots, grated
1½ teaspoons salt
Pepper to taste
Garlic juice to taste
1 cup cooked rice
5 tablespoons (or more) milk
2 eggs
3 slices bread, soaked in water
2 (16-ounce) cans sauerkraut
2 (8-ounce) cans tomato sauce
5 sauce cans water

- Place the cabbage in enough water to cover in a large saucepan. Bring to a boil over medium heat. Cook until the center is tender-crisp. Drain and cool slightly. Separate the leaves of the cabbage.
- Combine the pork, veal, beef, onions, parsley, carrots, salt, pepper, garlic juice, rice, milk, eggs and bread in a large bowl and mix well.
- Place a small amount of the pork mixture near the edge of each cabbage leaf and roll to enclose the filling. Place the cabbage rolls in a large roasting pan. Pour in the sauerkraut, tomato sauce and water.
- Bake at 325 degrees for 2½ hours.
- May use 1 can sauerkraut if using a small roasting pan.
- Yield: 56 cabbage rolls.

Friend of The Shipwreck Society

Main Dishes

Veal Casserole

1 pound veal, cut into small
    cubes
3 tablespoons flour
2 tablespoons vegetable oil
1½ cups chopped celery
2 small onions, chopped
1 (10-ounce) can cream of
    chicken soup
1 (10-ounce) can cream of
    mushroom soup
1 soup can water
2 tablespoons soy sauce
½ cup uncooked rice

- Toss the veal with the flour in a large bowl until coated.
- Brown the veal in hot oil in a large skillet, stirring to brown all sides.
- Combine the veal, celery, onions, soups, water, soy sauce and rice in a bowl and mix well. Spoon into a baking dish.
- Bake at 325 degrees for 2½ hours.
- May substitute pork for the veal.
- Yield: 4 servings.

Friend of The Shipwreck Society

Venison Herb Roast

1 (3- to 4-pound) venison roast
1 tablespoon vegetable oil
1/2 teaspoon salt
1/4 teaspoon pepper
1/4 cup flour
2 teaspoons marjoram
1 teaspoon thyme
2 teaspoons rosemary
1 clove of garlic, crushed
1 cup apple juice
1 cup water

- Pat the venison dry with paper towels. Cut several 1/2-inch deep slits in the venison. Rub with the oil and sprinkle with the salt and pepper.
- Combine the flour, marjoram, thyme, rosemary and garlic in a bowl and mix well. Coat the surface of the venison with the mixture and stuff into the slits. Place the venison in a large roasting pan. Do not use a rack. Pour in the apple juice and water.
- Bake, uncovered, at 350 degrees for 2 hours or until a meat thermometer registers 160 degrees for medium or 170 degrees for well done, basting frequently with the pan drippings.
- Note: Wild meat has a better flavor if soaked in salted water for several hours before cooking. Rinse with clear water and omit salt in the recipe.
- Yield: 6 servings.

Friend of The Shipwreck Society

Main Dishes

Venison Pepper Steak

1 pound venison steak, thinly
   cut
1 tablespoon vegetable oil
1 beef bouillon cube
1½ cups boiling water
¾ teaspoon salt
4 teaspoons soy sauce
3 green bell peppers, chopped
1 cup chopped celery
¼ cup water
2 tablespoons cornstarch
4 teaspoons molasses

- Cut the venison into strips. Sauté the venison in the oil in a large skillet.
- Dissolve the bouillon cube in the boiling water in a saucepan. Add the salt and soy sauce and mix well. Add the venison. Cover and bring to a boil over medium heat. Simmer over low heat for 10 minutes, stirring occasionally. Add the green peppers and celery. Simmer for 10 minutes.
- Combine ¼ cup water and cornstarch in a bowl and mix well. Stir in the molasses. Add to the venison and mix well. Cook for 2 minutes longer, stirring frequently. Serve with rice or noodles.
- Yield: 4 servings.

Anna Carlson

Venison Sandwich

Venison roast sandwiches were sliced meat and sliced Bermuda onions or pickles, along with mustard or catsup or Mother's mayonnaise.

Chicken-Fried Venison

Venison steaks or chops
Flour
Bacon drippings
Sliced potatoes
Salt and pepper to taste

- Pound the venison with a meat mallet. Coat with flour and pound again. Place bacon drippings in 2 cast-iron skillets. Fry the venison in 1 skillet, turning to brown both sides. Remove to a hot platter and keep warm in the oven.
- Sprinkle the potatoes with salt and pepper. Fry the potatoes in the second skillet until the venison is removed. Transfer the potatoes to the venison skillet to complete browning in the venison drippings, stirring constantly. Spoon onto the platter with the venison.
- Yield: variable

Anna Carlson

Main Dishes

Tomato Steak Venison

2 to 3 round venison steaks
Flour
Salt and pepper to taste
Potatoes, cut into halves
Onions, sliced
Carrots, cut into chunks
1 to 2 (16-ounce) cans
   tomatoes
Crisp-fried bacon slices

- Pound the venison with a meat mallet. Cut into serving pieces. Coat with a mixture of flour, salt and pepper. Place in a roasting pan.
- Add the potatoes, onions and carrots to the venison. Pour in the tomatoes.
- Bake at 350 degrees until done to taste. Place the venison on a serving platter. Top with the bacon.
- Yield: variable.

Anna Carlson

Venison Goulash

1½ pounds venison, cut into
   1x1-inch cubes
2 tablespoons vegetable oil
3 medium onions, thinly sliced
2 tablespoons paprika
1 teaspoon salt
1 medium green bell pepper,
   thinly sliced
½ cup water

- Sauté the venison in the oil in a large skillet. Add the onions and sprinkle with the paprika and salt. Sauté over medium heat until the onions are tender. Add the green pepper and water. Simmer, covered, over low heat for 1 to 1½ hours or until the venison is fork tender. Serve over wide egg noodles.
- Yield: 6 servings.

Friend of The Shipwreck Society

Main Dishes

Ground Venison Casserole

6 cups sliced potatoes
2 medium onions, sliced
2 tablespoons butter
1 pound ground venison
6 slices American cheese
1 (10-ounce) can cream of
    mushroom soup
2 cups milk
1 teaspoon salt
1/4 teaspoon pepper

- Place the potatoes in a saucepan with enough water to cover. Bring to a boil over medium heat and drain.
- Sauté the onions in the butter in a skillet for 2 minutes. Add the venison. Cook until brown, stirring occasionally.
- Layer 1/2 of the potatoes, venison, cheese and remaining 1/2 of the potatoes in a buttered baking dish.
- Combine the soup, milk, salt and pepper in a saucepan. Bring to a boil over medium heat, stirring frequently. Pour over the layers.
- Bake, covered, at 375 degrees for 1 hour. Remove the cover. Bake for 30 minutes longer.
- Yield: 8 servings.

Friend of The Shipwreck Society

Main Dishes

Upper Peninsula Venison Liver

Venison liver
1 large onion, sliced
1¼ tablespoons olive oil
1 tablespoon butter
Salt and pepper to taste
Lemon juice to taste

- Cut the venison liver into thin slices. Place in a saucepan with enough water to cover. Bring to a boil over medium heat and drain.
- Sauté the onion in the olive oil and butter in a skillet. Add the venison liver. Fry until light brown. Season with salt, pepper and lemon juice. Do not overcook or liver will be tough.
- Yield: variable.

Friend of The Shipwreck Society

Venison Salami

5 pounds ground venison
5 teaspoons Tender-Quick salt
3½ teaspoons garlic salt
2½ teaspoons hickory smoke salt
2½ teaspoons coarse ground pepper
3½ teaspoons mustard seeds
1 teaspoon celery seeds

- Combine the venison, Tender-Quick salt, garlic salt, smoke salt, pepper, mustard seeds and celery seeds in a bowl and mix well.
- Chill, covered, in the refrigerator for 3 days, removing to knead well 1 time each day.
- Knead well and shape into logs on the fourth day. Place on a rack in a broiler pan.
- Bake at 175 degrees for 8 hours.
- Yield: 20 servings.

Friend of The Shipwreck Society

Main Dishes

Venison Sausage

2 pounds ground venison
1¹/₂ tablespoons liquid smoke
1 cup cold water
3 tablespoons Tender-Quick
   salt
¹/₄ teaspoon garlic salt
¹/₄ teaspoon onion salt
¹/₄ cup mustard seeds

- Combine the venison, liquid smoke, cold water, Tender-Quick salt, garlic salt, onion salt and mustard seeds in a bowl and mix well. Shape into 2 rolls. Wrap each roll in foil, dull side out.
- Chill in the refrigerator for 24 hours.
- Pierce the foil wrap of the sausage rolls with a fork and place the rolls on a rack on a broiler pan. Pour ³/₄ cup water into the pan.
- Bake at 350 degrees for 1¹/₂ hours.
- Do not substitute regular salt for Tender-Quick salt.
- Yield: 8 servings.

Friend of The Shipwreck Society

Home First Aid

 Witch Hazel—For skin and bruises.
Baby Oil—Use on children up to ten years old to keep skin soft.

Main Dishes

Venison Sloppy Joes

2 pounds ground venison
1 cup chopped onion
1 cup finely diced celery
2 tablespoons bacon drippings
   or vegetable oil
1 clove of garlic, minced
1/2 cup barbecue sauce
2 tablespoons brown sugar
2 teaspoons dry mustard
1/2 cup catsup
1³/4 cups water
2 teaspoons salt
1/4 teaspoon pepper
1/4 cup vinegar
1 teaspoon paprika
2 teaspoons chili powder

- Brown the venison with the onion and celery in the bacon drippings in a skillet, stirring frequently. Spoon off the excess drippings.
- Combine the garlic, barbecue sauce, brown sugar, dry mustard, catsup, water, salt, pepper, vinegar, paprika and chili powder in a bowl and mix well. Pour over the venison. Simmer, covered, for 1 hour over low heat, stirring occasionally. Serve over hamburger buns.
- Yield: 8 servings.

Friend of The Shipwreck Society

Cranberry Meat Loaves

1¹/2 to 2 pounds ground
   venison
1/2 teaspoon salt
1 onion, finely chopped
1 or 2 eggs
1/4 pound ground ham
Pepper to taste
Bread crumbs
1/2 cup cranberry sauce

- Combine the venison, salt, onion, eggs, ham, pepper, bread crumbs and cranberry sauce in a bowl and mix well. Place in 2 loaf pans.
- Bake at 350 degrees for 1 to 1¹/2 hours or until cooked through.
- Yield: 6 to 8 servings.

Anna Carlson

Main Dishes

Venison Pork Sausage

1 pound ground venison
1 pound bulk pork sausage

- Combine the venison and pork sausage in a bowl and mix well. Shape into 8 patties.
- Fry in a skillet for 15 minutes on each side or until cooked through.
- Yield: 4 servings.

Friend of The Shipwreck Society

D.C.

Main Dishes

Pork Chops Florentine

6 loin pork chops, ³/₄ to 1 inch
   thick
Seasoned salt
2 (10-ounce) packages frozen
   spinach
3 tablespoons margarine
3 tablespoons flour
1 cup milk
1 teaspoon salt
¹/₈ teaspoon pepper
¹/₂ cup shredded Cheddar
   cheese
1 bottle mustard sauce

- Trim the fat from the pork chops. Fry the pork chops in a skillet until golden brown. Sprinkle with seasoned salt.
- Cook the spinach using the package directions and drain.
- Melt the margarine in a saucepan. Stir in the flour until well mixed. Add the milk, salt and pepper, mixing well. Add the cheese. Cook until thickened, stirring constantly. Stir in the spinach.
- Spoon the mixture into a greased casserole. Arrange the pork chops on top.
- Bake, covered, at 350 degrees for 30 minutes. Remove the cover. Bake for 15 minutes longer. Serve with the mustard sauce.
- Yield: 6 servings.

Friend of The Shipwreck Society

Main Dishes

Brimley Breakfast Casserole

8 ounces regular bulk sausage
8 ounces spicy bulk sausage
6 eggs
2 cups milk
1 teaspoon salt
2 slices bread, torn into pieces
1 cup shredded Cheddar cheese
1 teaspoon dry mustard

- Brown the sausage in a skillet, stirring until crumbly; drain well.
- Combine the eggs, milk and salt in a large bowl and beat well. Add the bread, cheese, mustard and sausage and mix well. Pour into a greased 9x13-inch baking dish.
- Chill, covered, for 8 to 10 hours. Remove the cover.
- Bake at 350 degrees for 45 to 55 minutes or until cooked through.
- Yield: 10 servings.

Michele Bergeron

Main Dishes

Lake Superior Fish Boil

2 gallons water
4 ounces salt
2 to 3 pounds small red
  potatoes
8 to 10 small onions
4 ounces salt
2 to 3 pounds whitefish, cut
  into 2-inch chunks

- Combine the water and 4 ounces salt in a large saucepan. Bring to a boil.
- Add the potatoes. Boil for 15 minutes, stirring occasionally.
- Add the onions. Boil for 5 minutes, stirring occasionally.
- Add the remaining 4 ounces salt and the fish. Boil for 10 minutes, stirring occasionally. Drain through a sieve. Garnish with lemon wedges and butter.
- Yield: variable.

Anna Carlson

Breading for Whitefish

2 cups breading mix
2 cups baking mix
3/4 cup grated Parmesan cheese
1 tablespoon onion soup mix
1 tablespoon paprika
1 tablespoon Italian seasoning
1 tablespoon dried parsley
  flakes
1 teaspoon garlic powder

- Combine the breading mix, baking mix, cheese, onion soup mix, paprika, Italian seasoning, parsley flakes and garlic powder in a bowl and mix well. Store in a large sealable plastic bag in the refrigerator.
- May add salt and pepper to taste.
- Yield: 4 cups.

Anna Carlson

Main Dishes

Main Dishes

Crusty Baked Whitefish

1 1/2 pounds fillet of whitefish
1/8 cup lemon juice
1/4 cup finely chopped onion
1 egg, beaten
3 tablespoons boiling water
Salt and pepper to taste
2 1/2 cups slightly crushed
   cornflakes
1/2 cup chopped fresh parsley
1/4 cup melted butter
Paprika

- Place the whitefish in an 8x8-inch baking dish.
- Combine the lemon juice, onion, egg, boiling water, salt, pepper, cornflake crumbs, parsley and butter in a bowl and mix well. Spread over the whitefish. Sprinkle with paprika.
- Bake at 375 degrees for 30 to 35 minutes or until the fish flakes easily.
- Yield: 4 servings.

Friend of The Shipwreck Society

Fish Sandwich

One day Mother took some cold leftover whitefish and added some chopped onion, a bit of chopped dill, and her mayonnaise, and we had fish sandwiches. Good.

Main Dishes

Baked Whitefish with Lemon Mushroom Sauce

1 (10-ounce) can cream of
    mushroom soup
$^1\!/_2$ cup milk
1 (4-ounce) can sliced
    mushrooms
1 large onion, chopped
2 tablespoons lemon juice
1 teaspoon paprika
$^1\!/_2$ teaspoon salt
$^1\!/_4$ teaspoon oregano
$^1\!/_4$ teaspoon pepper
1 bay leaf, crushed
2 to 3 pounds whitefish
Poultry seasoning
1 cup buttered bread crumbs
Butter

- Combine the soup, milk, mushrooms, onion, lemon juice, paprika, salt, oregano, pepper and crushed bay leaf in a saucepan. Simmer over low heat for 10 minutes, stirring occasionally.
- Place the whitefish in a buttered shallow baking dish. Pour the sauce over the fish.
- Combine a small amount of poultry seasoning and the buttered bread crumbs in a bowl and mix well. Sprinkle over the fish. Dot with butter.
- Bake at 375 degrees for 45 minutes.
- Yield: 6 servings.

Friend of The Shipwreck Society

Smoked Fish Spread

12 ounces smoked boneless
    skinless whitefish, flaked
8 ounces cream cheese, softened
2 tablespoons Dijon mustard
2 tablespoons mayonnaise

- Combine the whitefish, cream cheese, mustard and mayonnaise in a bowl and mix well.
- Chill, covered, for 24 hours or longer before serving.
- Yield: 2 cups.

Mitzi Robertson

Main Dishes

Italian Fish Patties

1 pound salmon
Salt and pepper to taste
1 cup bread crumbs
1/2 cup grated Italian cheese
2 eggs, beaten
1 teaspoon garlic powder
1/2 teaspoon basil
1 teaspoon chopped parsley

- Combine the salmon, salt, pepper, bread crumbs, cheese, eggs, garlic powder, basil and parsley in a bowl and mix well. Shape into patties.
- Fry the patties in a skillet, turning to brown both sides.
- Yield: 6 to 8 patties.

Friend of the Shipwreck Society

Tartar Sauce for Fish

1/4 cup minced sweet pickles
1/2 cup homemade mayonnaise
2 tablespoons grated onion

- Combine the pickles, mayonnaise and onion in a bowl and mix well. Serve with fish.
- Yield: about 3/4 cup.

Cecelia Carlson Endress

Main Dishes

Chicken Casserole

8 ounces fresh mushrooms
¹/₂ cup butter
1 (8-ounce) can water
    chestnuts, drained
7 slices white bread
5 whole chicken breasts,
    cooked, chopped
8 slices sharp Cheddar cheese,
    grated
4 eggs
1¹/₂ cups milk
¹/₂ teaspoon salt
1 (10-ounce) can cream of
    celery soup
1 (10-ounce) can cream of
    mushroom soup
¹/₂ cup mayonnaise
1 (2-ounce) jar chopped
    pimento

- Sauté the mushrooms in the butter in a skillet for about 10 minutes. Add the water chestnuts and mix well.
- Layer the bread, chicken, mushroom mixture and cheese in a greased 3-quart baking dish.
- Combine the eggs, milk and salt in a bowl and beat well. Pour over the layers.
- Combine the soups, mayonnaise and pimento in a bowl and mix well. Pour over the layers.
- Chill, covered, for 8 to 10 hours.
- Bake at 350 degrees for 1¹/₂ hours.
- Yield: 10 servings.

Friend of the Shipwreck Society

Duck Sandwich

One day Mother took some cold duck, sliced it and put it between two slices of bread, and topped the duck with cranberry sauce and some of her famous mayonnaise. It was real good. The same idea can be used with either chicken or turkey.

Main Dishes

Chicken Noodle Bake

½ (16-ounce) package egg
    noodles
1 cup finely chopped celery
¼ cup finely chopped onion
3 tablespoons butter or
    margarine
1 (10-ounce) can cream of
    chicken soup
¾ cup milk
2 cups shredded Cheddar
    cheese
1 (16-ounce) can diced
    carrots, drained
1 (4-ounce) can sliced
    mushrooms, drained
1½ cups chopped cooked
    chicken
½ teaspoon salt
½ teaspoon pepper
½ cup buttered bread crumbs

- Prepare the egg noodles using the package directions and drain.
- Sauté the celery and onion in the butter in a saucepan until tender. Add the soup, milk and cheese. Cook until the cheese is melted, stirring constantly.
- Combine the cheese sauce, noodles, carrots, mushrooms, chicken, salt and pepper in a bowl and mix well. Pour into a 3-quart baking dish. Top with the bread crumbs.
- Bake at 350 degrees for 30 minutes. Store leftovers in the refrigerator.
- May substitute turkey for chicken.
- Yield: 6 servings.

Jan M. Holt

Chicken and Noodle Casserole

4 ounces noodles
1 quart boiling water
1 tablespoon salt
3 tablespoons vegetable oil
3 tablespoons flour
1 teaspoon salt
1/4 teaspoon paprika
1 cup chicken stock
1 cup milk
1/4 cup olives, chopped
2 cups cubed cooked chicken
1 tablespoon lemon juice

- Cook the noodles using package directions in 1 quart boiling water and 1 tablespoon salt in a saucepan; drain if needed.
- Combine the oil, flour, salt and paprika in a bowl and mix until smooth. Add the chicken stock and milk gradually, mixing well. Add the olives, chicken, lemon juice and noodles and mix well. Pour into a 1 1/2-quart casserole.
- Bake, covered, at 350 degrees for 45 minutes. Serve hot.
- Yield: 6 servings.

Friend of The Shipwreck Society

Jack's Favorite Chicken and Rice

1 3/4 cups uncooked rice
1 (10-ounce) can cream of
  mushroom soup
1 (10-ounce) can cream of
  chicken soup
1 (10-ounce) can cream of
  celery soup
2 1/2 cups water
4 chicken breasts or fryer pieces
1 envelope dry onion soup mix

- Combine the rice, soups and water in a large bowl and mix well. Pour into a large casserole.
- Rinse the chicken and pat dry. Arrange the chicken on top of the rice mixture. Sprinkle with the onion soup mix.
- Bake, covered, at 350 degrees for 2 hours.
- Yield: 4 servings.

Betty Holt

Main Dishes

BREADS

...In the lighthouse kitchen, over a steaming hot stove, Grandmother was getting dinner for the men. She had gotten up at 5:00 a.m. and baked nine loaves of bread, followed by six apple pies. Then she made up cookie dough so that she could make cookies for the boys' evening lunch....

Indian Fry Bread

4 cups self-rising flour
3 tablespoons sugar
1½ cups milk
Vegetable oil for deep-frying

- Combine the flour and sugar in a bowl. Add the milk and mix well.
- Roll out ½ inch thick on a floured surface. Cut into desired shapes and cut a slit in the center.
- Deep-fry in hot oil until golden brown.
- Yield: 24 servings.

Friend of The Shipwreck Society

Blueberry Bran Muffins

1½ cups bran cereal
1 cup buttermilk
1 egg, beaten
¼ cup vegetable oil
1 cup flour
2 teaspoons baking powder
½ teaspoon baking soda
⅓ cup packed brown sugar
Dash of salt
1 cup blueberries

- Combine the cereal and buttermilk in a bowl. Let stand for 2 to 3 minutes. Add the egg and oil and mix well.
- Mix the flour, baking powder and baking soda in a bowl. Stir in the brown sugar and salt. Add the cereal mixture all at once, stirring briefly. Fold in the blueberries. Fill the greased muffin cups ⅔ full.
- Bake at 400 degrees for 20 to 30 minutes or until brown and the muffins test done.
- Yield: 12 servings.

Bertha Endress Rollo

Breads

Oatmeal Blueberry Muffins

1/2 cup shortening
2/3 cup packed brown sugar
2 eggs, lightly beaten
2 cups rolled oats
4 cups flour
4 teaspoons baking powder
1 1/2 teaspoons baking soda
1 tablespoon salt
2 1/2 cups buttermilk
2 cups blueberries

- Cream the shortening and brown sugar in a mixer bowl until light and fluffy. Beat in the eggs. Add the oats and beat well.
- Sift the flour, baking powder, baking soda and salt together. Add to the creamed mixture alternately with the buttermilk, mixing well after each addition.
- Stir in the blueberries. Fill greased muffin cups 2/3 full.
- Bake at 400 degrees for 20 to 25 minutes or until the muffins test done.
- Yield: 18 servings.

Friend of The Shipwreck Society

Breads

Cranberry Muffins

1 cup cranberries, coarsely
    chopped
1/4 to 1/3 cup sugar
1 3/4 cups flour
2 1/2 teaspoons baking powder
1/4 cup sugar
3/4 teaspoon salt
1 egg, beaten
3/4 cup milk
1/3 cup melted shortening or oil

- Combine the cranberries and 1/4 to 1/3 cup sugar in a bowl. Mix well and let stand for several minutes.
- Sift the flour, baking powder, 1/4 cup sugar and salt into a bowl. Make a well in the center. Add the egg, milk, shortening and cranberry mixture, stirring just until mixed. Fill greased muffin cups 2/3 full.
- Bake at 400 degrees for 20 to 25 minutes or until the muffins test done. Dip in melted butter and then in sugar while still warm.
- Yield: 12 servings.

Cecelia Carlson Endress

Home First Aid

 Wood Ashes—To make soap.
Ginger (ground)—To make stomach happy.

Breads

Cranberry Apple Muffins

1 cup all-purpose flour
1/2 cup whole wheat flour
1 teaspoon baking soda
1 teaspoon cinnamon
1/4 teaspoon nutmeg
1/8 teaspoon cloves
1/4 teaspoon salt
2 eggs
3/4 cup packed brown sugar
1/4 cup vegetable oil
1 teaspoon vanilla extract
3/4 cup finely chopped
    unpeeled apple
3/4 cup dried cranberries
1/2 cup chopped walnuts

- Combine the all-purpose flour, whole wheat flour, baking soda, cinnamon, nutmeg, cloves and salt in a bowl and mix well.
- Whisk the eggs and brown sugar together in a bowl. Add the oil and vanilla, whisking until smooth. Stir in the apple, cranberries and walnuts. Pour into the flour mixture, folding together just until mixed. Fill greased muffin cups 3/4 full.
- Bake at 350 degrees for 20 to 25 minutes or until the muffins test done.
- Yield: 12 servings.

Christel Goese

Breads

Finnish Cardamom Coffee Bread (Pulla)

1 envelope dry yeast
1/2 cup warm water
3 eggs, beaten
1 cup sugar
2 cups milk, scalded, cooled
1 teaspoon salt
10 cardamom seeds, crushed
6 to 7 cups flour
1/2 cup butter, softened

- Dissolve the yeast in the warm water.
- Beat the eggs and sugar in a mixer bowl. Add the cooled milk, yeast, salt and cardamom seeds and mix well. Beat in enough flour to make a thick batter. Let stand for 30 minutes.
- Add enough of the remaining flour to make a stiff dough, mixing well. Knead the butter into the dough. Let rise, covered, in a warm place until doubled in bulk.
- Punch the dough down on a floured surface. Separate into 3 portions. Roll each portion into a rope and braid. Place on a baking sheet. Let rise until doubled in bulk.
- Bake at 375 degrees for 30 minutes or until the bread tests done.
- Yield: 12 servings.

Friend of The Shipwreck Society

Breads

Graham Bread

1 tablespoon shortening
½ cup sugar
1 teaspoon salt
2 cups sour milk
2 teaspoons baking soda
1 cup all-purpose flour
3 cups graham flour

- Combine the shortening and sugar in a mixer bowl and beat well. Add the salt, milk and baking soda and beat well. Stir in the all-purpose flour and graham flour until a stiff batter forms. Pour into a greased loaf pan.
- Bake at 350 degrees for 1 hour or until the bread tests done.
- Yield: 12 servings.

Friend of The Shipwreck Society

Peanut Butter Sandwich

 In those days we bought peanut butter in pails or cans. It was not mixed and you had to stir and stir to get the oil mixed in. Grandmother never allowed us to have jelly or jam on it. To her, peanut butter was enough.

Breads

Whole Wheat Bread

5 cups all-purpose flour
2 envelopes dry yeast
2³/₄ cups water
¹/₂ cup packed brown sugar
¹/₄ cup shortening
1 tablespoon salt
3 cups whole wheat flour
¹/₂ to ³/₄ cup raisins, chopped
   or coarsely ground

- Combine 3¹/₂ cups of the all-purpose flour and yeast in a large bowl.
- Combine the water, brown sugar, shortening and salt in a saucepan. Heat over medium heat until the shortening is melted, stirring frequently. Add to the flour mixture and beat well. Stir in the whole wheat flour and enough of the remaining all-purpose flour to make a stiff dough. Add the raisins. Knead for 10 to 12 minutes or until the dough is smooth. Place the dough in a greased bowl, turning to grease all surfaces. Let rise, covered, for 1 hour or until doubled in bulk.
- Punch the dough down. Divide into 2 portions on a floured surface. Let rest for several minutes. Shape into loaves and place in 2 greased loaf pans. Let rise, covered, until doubled in bulk.
- Bake at 375 degrees for 40 to 45 minutes or until the bread tests done.
- Cool in the pans for several minutes. Remove to a wire rack to cool completely.
- May cover the bread with foil for the last 5 minutes of baking if browning too fast.
- Yield: 24 servings.

Anna Carlson

Breads

Blueberry Nut Bread

1³/₄ cups milk
2 eggs
¹/₂ cup melted butter or
    margarine
1¹/₂ cups white or brown sugar
2 tablespoons baking powder
1 teaspoon salt
5 cups flour
2 cups blueberries
¹/₂ cup chopped nuts

- Combine the milk, eggs and butter in a bowl and mix well.
- Sift the sugar, baking powder, salt and flour together. Add to the milk mixture and mix well.
- Combine the blueberries and nuts in a bowl. Fold into the batter. Pour into a greased loaf pan. Let stand for 15 to 20 minutes.
- Bake at 350 degrees for 1 hour.
- Yield: 12 servings.

Friend of The Shipwreck Society

Breads

Blueberry Banana Bread

1 cup fresh blueberries
1³/₄ cups flour
2 teaspoons baking powder
¹/₄ teaspoon baking soda
¹/₂ teaspoon salt
¹/₃ cup butter, softened
²/₃ cup sugar
2 eggs
1 cup mashed ripe bananas

- Rinse the blueberries and drain. Combine the blueberries and 2 tablespoons of the flour in a bowl and toss to coat.
- Sift the remaining flour, baking powder, baking soda and salt together.
- Cream the butter in a mixer bowl. Add the sugar and beat until light and fluffy. Beat in the eggs 1 at a time. Add the flour mixture and bananas gradually in 3 portions, mixing well after each addition. Stir in the blueberries. Spoon into a greased 5x9-inch loaf pan.
- Bake at 350 degrees for 50 minutes or until the bread tests done.
- Cool in the pan for several minutes. Remove to a wire rack to cool completely.
- Yield: 12 servings.

Bertha Endress Rollo

Breads

Blueberry Lemon Bread

6 tablespoons butter, softened
1 cup sugar
2 eggs
2 cups (about) flour
1 tablespoon baking powder
1/4 teaspoon salt
1/2 cup milk
1 cup fresh blueberries
1 tablespoon grated lemon
    peel and lemon juice

- Cream the butter and sugar in a mixer bowl until light and fluffy. Beat in the eggs 1 at a time.
- Sift the flour, baking powder and salt together. Add alternately with the milk to the egg mixture, mixing well after each addition. Stir in the blueberries, lemon peel and lemon juice. Pour into a greased and floured loaf pan.
- Bake at 350 degrees for 1 hour. Cool in the pan for several minutes. Remove to a wire rack to cool completely.
- Yield: 12 servings.

Christel Goese

Breads

Cranberry Orange Bread

2 cups flour
1 cup sugar
1½ teaspoons baking powder
½ teaspoon baking soda
½ teaspoon salt
2 tablespoons shortening
¾ cup orange juice and
   grated peel
1 egg, beaten
1 cup fresh cranberries, cut
   into halves

- Combine the flour, sugar, baking powder, baking soda and salt in a bowl and mix well. Add the shortening, orange juice and peel and egg; mix well. Fold in the cranberries. Pour into a greased 5x9-inch loaf pan.
- Bake at 350 degrees for 1 hour.
- Cool in the pan for several minutes. Remove to a wire rack to cool completely.
- Yield: 12 servings.

Bertha Endress Rollo

Home First Aid

 Calamine—Lotion for insect bites.
Baking Soda—For brushing teeth and as a gargle.

Breads

Hungarian Coffee Cake

2¼ cups flour
1 teaspoon baking powder
1 teaspoon baking soda
½ teaspoon salt
¼ cup shortening
1 cup sugar
2 eggs
¾ cup apple butter
1 teaspoon vanilla extract
1 cup sour cream
Streusel

- Sift the flour, baking powder, baking soda and salt together.
- Cream the shortening in a mixer bowl. Add the sugar and beat until light and fluffy. Beat in the eggs 1 at a time. Add the apple butter and vanilla and beat well. Add the flour mixture alternately with the sour cream, beating well after each addition. Pour ½ of the batter into a greased and floured 9x13-inch baking dish. Sprinkle on the Streusel. Top with the remaining batter.
- Bake at 350 degrees for 35 to 40 minutes or until the coffee cake tests done.

Streusel

1 cup sugar
1 tablespoon flour
2 teaspoons cinnamon
1 teaspoon nutmeg
2 tablespoons butter

- Combine the sugar, flour, cinnamon and nutmeg in a bowl and mix well. Cut in the butter until crumbly.
- Yield: 15 servings.

Friend of The Shipwreck Society

Breads

Zucchini Bread

3 eggs
1 cup vegetable oil
2 cups sugar
2 cups flour
½ teaspoon baking powder
1 teaspoon salt
2 teaspoons baking soda
1 tablespoon cinnamon
1 tablespoon vanilla extract
1 cup chopped nuts
1 cup raisins
2 cups grated unpeeled
  zucchini

- Beat the eggs in a mixer bowl. Add the oil and sugar and beat well.
- Mix the flour, baking powder, salt, baking soda and cinnamon together. Add to the egg mixture. Add the vanilla and beat well. Stir in the nuts, raisins and zucchini. Pour into 2 greased loaf pans.
- Bake at 350 degrees for 50 to 60 minutes or until the bread tests done.
- Cool in the pans for several minutes. Remove to a wire rack to cool completely.
- Yield: 24 servings.

Friend of The Shipwreck Society

Breads

Finnish Pancakes (Plattyja)

2 eggs
1 tablespoon sugar
3 cups milk
1½ cups flour
1 teaspoon salt
2 tablespoons melted butter

- Beat the eggs and sugar in a mixer bowl. Add the milk, flour and salt and beat well. Add the butter and mix well. The batter will be thin.
- Pour ¼ cup at a time onto a hot greased griddle. Bake until bubbles appear on the surface and the underside is brown. Turn the pancakes over. Bake until golden brown. Serve with syrup.
- Yield: 8 servings.

Friend of The Shipwreck Society

Highbanks Lake Pancakes

2 cups flour
4 teaspoons baking powder
1 teaspoon baking soda
Pinch of salt
2 tablespoons sugar
2 eggs, beaten
¼ cup vegetable oil
2 to 3 cups buttermilk

- Combine the flour, baking powder, baking soda, salt and sugar in a bowl and mix well. Combine the eggs and oil in a bowl. Add to the flour mixture and mix well. Add 2 cups buttermilk and enough of the remaining 1 cup buttermilk to make the batter of the desired consistency. Less buttermilk makes thicker pancakes.
- Bake on a hot greased griddle until brown, turning once.
- Yield: twenty 4-inch pancakes.

Gilbert Peterman

Breads

DESSERTS

*...Grandmother always brought
a freezer full of ice cream and a huge
bowl of mashed strawberries for topping.
I still insist that the ice cream was
the best I have ever tasted.
The ice cream was hand-churned
and I know—for many a time I gladly
turned the crank. The ice came from the
icehouse and the strawberries from
Granddad's garden....*

Blueberry Crisp

3 cups fresh blueberries or 16
  ounces frozen unsweetened
  blueberries
2 tablespoons lemon juice
2/3 cup packed brown sugar
1/2 cup flour
1/2 cup quick-cooking oats
1/3 cup butter or margarine,
  softened
3/4 teaspoon cinnamon
1/4 teaspoon salt

- Arrange the blueberries in an ungreased 8x8-inch baking dish. Sprinkle with the lemon juice.
- Mix the brown sugar, flour, oats, butter, cinnamon and salt in a bowl. Sprinkle over the blueberries.
- Bake at 375 degrees for 30 minutes or until the topping is light brown and the blueberries are hot.
- Serve with cream or ice cream.
- Yield: 4 to 6 servings.

Roxanne McKiddie

Blueberry Crumb Pudding

1 cup dry bread crumbs
1/4 cup sugar
1/4 teaspoon cinnamon
3 tablespoons melted butter
2 cups fresh blueberries
Whipped topping

- Combine the bread crumbs, sugar and cinnamon in a bowl and mix well. Stir in the butter until well mixed.
- Alternate layers of the blueberries and the crumb mixture in a small greased casserole 1/2 at a time, ending with the crumb mixture. Press down firmly with a spoon.
- Bake at 350 degrees for 30 minutes.
- Serve warm with whipped topping.
- Yield: 4 to 6 servings.

Friend of The Shipwreck Society

Desserts

Blueberry Cheesecake Tortes

2 tablespoons tapioca
1/2 cup sugar
1/3 cup water
2 cups blueberries
24 vanilla wafers
16 ounces cream cheese,
   softened
2 eggs
3/4 cup sugar
1 1/2 teaspoons vanilla extract
1/4 teaspoon salt

- Combine the tapioca, 1/2 cup sugar and water in a saucepan and mix well. Stir in the blueberries and let stand for 5 minutes. Cook over medium heat just until the mixture starts to thicken, stirring constantly. Cool slightly.
- Place the vanilla wafers in paper-lined muffin cups. Combine the cream cheese, eggs, remaining 3/4 cup sugar, vanilla and salt in a bowl and mix well. Place 1 heaping tablespoonful in each muffin cup. Top with the blueberry mixture.
- Bake at 375 degrees for 12 to 15 minutes. Place the muffin pans on wire racks to cool before removing tortes from cups. Store in the refrigerator.
- Yield: 24 servings.

Friend of The Shipwreck Society

Desserts

Cranberry and Apple Cobbler

$^1/_3$ cup sugar
1 tablespoon cornstarch
$^1/_2$ cup light corn syrup
$1^1/_2$ cups cranberries
2 apples, peeled, cored, sliced
Oat Topping

- Combine the sugar and cornstarch in a medium saucepan and mix well. Stir in the corn syrup until well mixed. Add the cranberries.
- Bring to a boil over medium heat, stirring frequently. Simmer over low heat until the cranberries pop open, stirring frequently. Stir in the apples. Pour the mixture into a greased 9-inch square baking dish.
- Crumble the Oat Topping over the fruit.
- Bake at 400 degrees for 30 to 35 minutes or until the topping is golden brown.

Oat Topping

$^3/_4$ cup flour
$^1/_2$ cup sugar
$^1/_3$ cup margarine
1 cup rolled oats
$^1/_4$ teaspoon vanilla or
   almond extract
1 egg, beaten

- Combine the flour and sugar in a bowl and mix well. Cut in the margarine until crumbly.
- Stir in the oats. Add the vanilla and egg and mix well.
- Yield: 8 servings.

Friend of The Shipwreck Society

Baked Cranberry Pudding

2 cups flour
1 cup sugar
2 1/2 teaspoons baking powder
3 tablespoons melted
  shortening
2/3 cup milk
1 egg
2 cups cranberries
Hot Butter Sauce

- Sift the flour, sugar and baking powder into a mixer bowl. Add the shortening, milk and egg. Beat for 2 minutes. Stir in the cranberries. Pour into a buttered 9-inch square baking dish.
- Bake at 350 degrees for 40 minutes. Cut into 3-inch squares. Serve with Hot Butter Sauce.
- Yield: 9 squares.

Hot Butter Sauce

1/2 cup butter
1 cup sugar
3/4 cup light cream or milk

- Melt the butter in a double boiler over hot water. Add the sugar and light cream.
- Cook over medium heat for 5 minutes, stirring occasionally.
- Yield: 2 cups.

Friend of The Shipwreck Society

Home First Aid

 Borax—For stinky shoes.
Matches—Quick air cleaner.

Desserts

Cream Puffs with Coffee Filling

½ cup butter
1 cup water
1 cup flour
4 eggs
Coffee Filling

- Combine the butter and water in a saucepan. Bring to a boil over medium heat. Add the flour, stirring until smooth. Remove from the heat. Beat in the eggs 1 at a time. Drop by spoonfuls onto a greased baking sheet.
- Bake at 375 degrees for 40 to 45 minutes or until light brown.
- Cool on a wire rack. Cut off the tops and remove the soft dough inside. Fill with the cool Coffee Filling.

Coffee Filling

2 eggs, beaten
2 tablespoons cornstarch
1 cup sugar
2 cups milk, scalded
¼ cup coffee
½ teaspoon vanilla extract

- Combine the eggs, cornstarch and sugar in a double boiler and mix well. Add the milk.
- Cook over hot water over medium heat until thickened, stirring constantly. Stir in the coffee and vanilla. Cool the filling.
- Yield: 10 to 12 servings.

Cecelia Carlson Endress

Desserts

Canadian Maple Mousse

6 egg yolks
1/8 teaspoon salt
3/4 cup maple syrup
2 cups whipping cream,
    whipped
1 cup crushed peanut brittle

- Combine the egg yolks, salt and maple syrup in a double boiler and mix well. Cook over hot water over medium heat until the mixture is thickened and coats a spoon, stirring constantly. Pour into a mixer bowl.
- Beat until the mixture is cooled. Fold in the whipped cream. Fold in 1/2 of the crushed peanut brittle. Pour into a glass dish. Sprinkle with the remaining 1/2 cup crushed peanut brittle.
- Freeze until 30 minutes before serving.
- Yield: 6 to 8 servings.

Jill F. Peterman

Desserts

Wild Raspberry Mousse

2 tablespoons unflavored
  gelatin
1/2 cup cold water
1 cup sugar
1 cup water
2 1/2 cups wild raspberries
3 egg whites, stiffly beaten
1 cup heavy cream, whipped

- Soften the gelatin in 1/2 cup cold water in a bowl.
- Combine the sugar and 1 cup water in a saucepan. Cook over medium heat until the mixture reaches a full rolling boil, stirring occasionally.
- Reserve 1/2 cup of the raspberries. Add the remaining 2 cups raspberries to the syrup. Cook until the raspberries are soft, stirring frequently. Force the raspberries through a fine sieve, discarding the seeds.
- Add the hot raspberry purée to the gelatin, stirring until the gelatin dissolves. Chill until partially set.
- Fold the egg whites into the raspberry gelatin. Fold in 1/2 of the whipped cream. Pour the mousse into individual glasses or a serving bowl. Chill for 2 hours or until set. Chill the remaining whipped cream.
- Top the mousse with the remaining whipped cream and the reserved 1/2 cup raspberries.
- May be prepared 1 day before serving.
- Yield: 6 servings.

Friend of The Shipwreck Society

Desserts

Blueberry Sauce

½ cup sugar
2 tablespoons cornstarch
⅛ teaspoon salt
½ cup water
2 cups blueberries
1 teaspoon grated lemon peel
1 tablespoon lemon juice

- Combine the sugar, cornstarch and salt in a saucepan. Stir in the water until well mixed. Add the blueberries.
- Cook over medium heat for 5 minutes or until the liquid is clear and thickened, stirring frequently. Remove from the heat. Stir in the lemon peel and juice.
- Serve warm or cold over ice cream, custard, waffles or cake.
- Yield: 2 cups.

Christel Goese

Piimakakku (Finnish Buttermilk Cake)

2½ cups flour
1½ cups sugar
1½ teaspoons baking soda
1 teaspoon baking powder
¼ teaspoon salt
1 teaspoon cinnamon
½ teaspoon nutmeg
½ cup butter, softened
1½ cups buttermilk

- Combine the flour, sugar, baking soda, baking powder, salt, cinnamon and nutmeg in a large mixer bowl.
- Combine the butter and buttermilk in a bowl and mix well. Add to the dry ingredients and beat well. Pour into a greased bundt pan.
- Bake at 350 degrees for 50 minutes.
- Yield: 16 servings.

Friend of The Shipwreck Society

Desserts

Chocolate Pound Cake

1 cup butter, softened
1 cup margarine, softened
3 cups sugar
1/2 cup baking cocoa
5 eggs
3 cups flour
1/2 teaspoon salt
1/2 teaspoon baking powder
1 cup milk
1 tablespoon vanilla extract
Chocolate Glaze

- Cream the butter, margarine, sugar and cocoa in a mixer bowl until light and fluffy. Beat in the eggs 1 at a time.
- Sift the flour, salt and baking powder together. Add alternately with the milk and vanilla to the creamed mixture, mixing well after each addition. Pour into a greased and floured tube pan.
- Bake at 325 degrees for 1 1/2 hours.
- Cool in the pan for several minutes. Invert onto a serving plate. Cool the cake. Drizzle with Chocolate Glaze.

Chocolate Glaze

2 tablespoons baking cocoa
1/4 cup water
2 tablespoons light corn syrup
2 tablespoons butter
2 cups sifted confectioners'
    sugar

- Combine the cocoa and water in a saucepan and mix well. Add the corn syrup and butter.
- Cook over medium heat until the butter is melted, stirring constantly. Remove from the heat. Stir in the confectioners' sugar.
- Yield: 16 servings.

Friend of The Shipwreck Society

Desserts

"Even I Can Make It" Chocolate Cake

1 cup sugar
1/4 cup baking cocoa
6 tablespoons vegetable oil
1 1/2 cups flour
1/2 teaspoon salt
1 teaspoon baking soda
1 cup cold water
1 tablespoon white vinegar
2 teaspoons vanilla extract
Chocolate chips

- Cream the sugar, cocoa and oil in a mixer bowl until light and fluffy.
- Mix the flour, salt and baking soda together. Add to the creamed mixture and beat well. Add the cold water, vinegar and vanilla and mix well. Pour into a greased 9x9-inch cake pan.
- Bake at 350 degrees for 25 to 30 minutes or until the cake tests done. Sprinkle the hot cake with the chocolate chips, spreading to cover as the chocolate melts.
- Yield: 12 servings.

Jill F. Peterman

Orange Kiss-Me Cake

1 orange
⅓ cup sugar
1 cup raisins
⅓ cup walnuts
2 cups flour
1 cup sugar
1 teaspoon baking soda
1 teaspoon salt
2 teaspoons baking powder
½ cup shortening
¾ cup milk
2 eggs
¼ cup milk

- Squeeze the juice from the orange into a bowl, reserving the orange. Add ⅓ cup sugar to the orange juice. Let stand until needed, stirring occasionally.
- Grind the reserved orange, raisins and walnuts.
- Sift the flour, remaining 1 cup sugar, baking soda, salt and baking powder into a mixer bowl. Add the shortening and ¾ cup milk. Beat for 2 minutes.
- Combine the eggs and remaining ¼ cup milk in a bowl. Add to the batter and beat well. Fold in the ground mixture. Pour into a greased and floured tube pan.
- Bake at 350 degrees until the cake tests done.
- Cool in the pan for several minutes. Invert onto a serving plate. Pour the orange juice and sugar mixture over the warm cake.
- Yield: 16 servings.

Friend of The Shipwreck Society

Desserts

Date Squares

³/₄ cup chopped dates
1¹/₂ cups water
¹/₂ cup sugar
Date Square Topping

- Combine the dates, water and sugar in a saucepan. Cook over low heat for 10 minutes or until thickened, stirring constantly. Cool slightly.
- Layer ¹/₂ of the Date Square Topping in a greased baking dish, pressing firmly. Add the cooled date mixture, spreading to cover. Add the remaining ¹/₂ of the Date Square Topping, pressing with a spoon.
- Bake at 400 degrees for 20 to 30 minutes or until the dessert tests done.
- Cut into squares while hot.

Date Square Topping

³/₄ cup shortening
1 cup packed brown sugar
1³/₄ cups flour
¹/₂ teaspoon baking soda
1 teaspoon salt
1¹/₂ cups rolled oats

- Cream the shortening and brown sugar in a mixer bowl until light and fluffy.
- Mix the flour, baking soda and salt together. Add to the creamed mixture and mix well. Stir in the oats.
- Yield: 8 to 10 servings.

Helen Apostle Peterman

Desserts

Pumpkin Squares

24 single graham crackers,
  crushed
1/3 cup sugar
1/2 cup melted butter or
  margarine
2 eggs, beaten
3/4 cup sugar
8 ounces cream cheese, softened
1 (16-ounce) can pumpkin
3 egg yolks
1/2 cup sugar
1/2 cup milk
1/2 teaspoon salt
2 teaspoons cinnamon
1 envelope unflavored gelatin
1/4 cup cold water
3 egg whites
1/4 cup sugar
1 cup whipping cream
1 tablespoon sugar
1 teaspoon vanilla extract

- Combine the graham cracker crumbs, 1/3 cup sugar and butter in a bowl and mix well. Press the mixture into a buttered 9x13-inch baking dish.
- Combine the 2 eggs, 3/4 cup sugar and cream cheese in a mixer bowl. Beat until light and fluffy. Spread over the prepared crust. Bake at 350 degrees for 20 minutes.
- Combine the pumpkin, egg yolks, 1/2 cup sugar, milk, salt and cinnamon in a double boiler. Cook over boiling water for 5 minutes or until thickened, stirring frequently. Remove from the heat.
- Soften the gelatin in the cold water in a small saucepan. Heat over low heat just until dissolved, stirring constantly. Stir into the pumpkin mixture. Cool slightly.
- Beat the egg whites in a mixer bowl until soft peaks form. Add 1/4 cup sugar gradually, beating until stiff. Fold into the pumpkin mixture. Pour over the baked crust. Chill until serving time.
- Combine the whipping cream and 1 tablespoon sugar in a chilled mixer bowl. Beat until stiff, adding the vanilla while beating. Cut the dessert into squares. Top with the whipped cream.
- Yield: 15 servings.

Friend of The Shipwreck Society

Desserts

Cranberry Date Bars

1 (12-ounce) package fresh or
  frozen cranberries, thawed
1 (8-ounce) package chopped
  dates
2 tablespoons water
1 teaspoon vanilla extract
2 cups flour
2 cups rolled oats
1½ cups packed brown sugar
½ teaspoon baking soda
½ teaspoon salt
1 cup melted butter
Orange Glaze

- Combine the cranberries, dates and water in a saucepan. Simmer, covered, over low heat for 15 minutes or until the cranberries have popped, stirring occasionally. Remove from the heat. Stir in the vanilla. Cool slightly.
- Combine the flour, oats, brown sugar, baking soda and salt in a large bowl and mix well. Stir in the butter until well mixed. Press ½ of the mixture into an ungreased 9x13-inch baking dish.
- Bake at 350 degrees for 8 minutes.
- Spoon the cranberry mixture over the baked crust. Sprinkle with the remaining ½ of the flour mixture, pressing gently.
- Bake at 350 degrees for 25 to 30 minutes. Place the baking dish on a wire rack to cool. Drizzle with the Orange Glaze.

Orange Glaze

2 cups confectioners' sugar
2 to 3 tablespoons orange juice
½ teaspoon vanilla extract

- Combine the confectioners' sugar, orange juice and vanilla in a mixer bowl and beat well.
- Yield: 36 servings.

Jan M. Holt

Desserts

Double Fudge Brownies

1¹/₄ cups butter, softened
4 cups sugar
8 eggs
2 cups flour
1¹/₄ cups baking cocoa
1 teaspoon salt
2¹/₂ teaspoons vanilla extract
2 cups chopped walnuts or
    pecans
Chocolate Icing

- Cream the butter and sugar in a mixer bowl until light and fluffy. Beat in the eggs 1 at a time.
- Mix the flour, cocoa and salt together. Add to the creamed mixture and mix well. Stir in the vanilla and walnuts. Pour into a greased 10x15-inch baking dish.
- Bake at 325 degrees for 40 to 50 minutes or until the brownies test done.
- Cool for 10 minutes. Spread Chocolate Icing over the warm brownies. Garnish with additional chopped walnuts.

Chocolate Icing

¹/₂ cup butter
2 squares unsweetened
    chocolate
3 cups confectioners' sugar
5 tablespoons milk
1 teaspoon vanilla

- Combine the butter and chocolate in a saucepan. Heat over low heat until the mixture is melted, stirring frequently.
- Pour into a mixer bowl. Add ¹/₂ of the confectioners' sugar and beat well. Add milk, vanilla and remaining ¹/₂ of the confectioners' sugar and beat until smooth.
- Yield: 36 servings.

Jan M. Holt

Desserts

Toffee Bars

1 cup margarine, softened
1 teaspoon vanilla extract
1 cup packed brown sugar
2 cups flour
1 cup chocolate chips
1 cup nuts, chopped

- Cream the margarine, vanilla and brown sugar in a mixer bowl until light and fluffy. Add the flour and mix well. Stir in the chocolate chips and nuts. Press into a greased 9x13-inch baking pan.
- Bake at 350 degrees for 20 to 25 minutes or until light brown.
- Cut into bars. Cool in the baking pan before removing.
- Yield: 15 servings.

Friend of The Shipwreck Society

Desserts

Chocolate Chip Cookies

1 cup butter or margarine,
   softened
1 cup packed brown sugar
½ cup sugar
1 teaspoon vanilla extract
2 eggs
2¼ cups flour
1 teaspoon salt
1 teaspoon baking soda
1 cup chocolate chips

- Cream the butter, brown sugar, sugar and vanilla in a mixer bowl until light and fluffy. Beat in the eggs 1 at a time.
- Mix the flour, salt and baking soda together. Add to the creamed mixture and mix well. Stir in the chocolate chips. Drop by teaspoonfuls onto a greased cookie sheet.
- Bake at 350 degrees for 10 minutes.
- Cool on the cookie sheet for several minutes. Remove to a wire rack to cool completely.
- Yield: 30 servings.

Betty A. Holt

Desserts

Chocolate Cheese Drop Cookies

2 (1-ounce) squares
    unsweetened chocolate
1/2 cup butter, softened
1/2 cup shortening
3 ounces cream cheese, softened
1 egg
1/2 teaspoon salt
1 1/2 cups sugar
2 tablespoons milk
1 teaspoon vanilla extract
2 1/4 cups flour
1 1/2 teaspoons baking powder
1/2 cup chopped nuts

- Melt the chocolate in a double boiler over hot water.
- Cream the butter, shortening and cream cheese in a mixer bowl until light and fluffy. Add the egg, salt, sugar, milk and vanilla and beat well. Add the melted chocolate, flour and baking powder and mix well. Stir in the nuts. Drop by teaspoonfuls onto a greased cookie sheet.
- Bake at 350 degrees for 10 to 15 minutes or until light brown. Cool on the cookie sheet for several minutes. Remove to a wire rack to cool completely.
- Yield: 60 servings.

Friend of The Shipwreck Society

Home First Aid

 Vaseline—On babies' bottoms, on hands to keep them soft after washing dishes, to shine patent leather shoes.

Desserts

Grandmother's Date Cookies

¹/₂ cup sugar
¹/₂ cup butter, softened
1 egg
¹/₂ cup milk
3 cups flour
1 tablespoon baking powder
1 cup boiling water
¹/₄ cup sugar
1 cup chopped dates

- Cream ¹/₂ cup sugar and butter in a mixer bowl until light and fluffy. Add the egg and milk and mix well. Add the flour and baking powder and mix well.
- Roll out the dough ¹/₄ inch thick on a floured surface. Cut into circles with a glass or cookie cutter.
- Combine the boiling water, ¹/₄ cup sugar and dates in a bowl. Stir until the sugar is dissolved.
- Spoon a small amount of the date filling onto ¹/₂ of each circle. Fold the circle over to enclose the filling. Press the edge with a fork to seal. Cut a few vents in each and place on a cookie sheet.
- Bake at 375 degrees for 10 to 15 minutes or until brown.
- Cool on the cookie sheet for several minutes. Remove to a wire rack to cool completely.
- Yield: 36 servings.

Anna Carlson

Desserts

Michigan Cookies

1 cup packed brown sugar
½ cup butter or margarine,
  softened
1 egg, beaten
2 (1-ounce) squares
  unsweetened chocolate,
  melted
1¾ cups flour
¼ teaspoon baking soda
1 teaspoon baking powder
½ teaspoon salt
½ cup milk
½ cup nuts, chopped

- Cream the brown sugar and butter in a mixer bowl until light and fluffy. Add the egg and chocolate and beat well.
- Sift the flour, baking soda, baking powder and salt together. Add to the creamed mixture alternately with the milk, mixing well after each addition. Stir in the nuts. Drop by teaspoonfuls 3 inches apart on a greased cookie sheet.
- Bake at 325 degrees for 8 to 10 minutes or until light brown.
- Cool on the cookie sheet for several minutes. Remove to a wire rack to cool completely.
- May add frosting if desired.
- Yield: 60 servings.

Friend of The Shipwreck Society

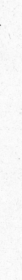

Granddad's Favorite Molasses Cookies

1½ cups sugar
1 cup shortening
1 egg
1 cup molasses
1 cup sour cream
1 tablespoon baking soda
2 tablespoons vinegar
4½ cups flour
1 teaspoon salt
2 teaspoons cinnamon
1 teaspoon ginger

- Cream the sugar and shortening in a mixer bowl until light and fluffy. Add the egg, molasses and sour cream and beat well.
- Combine the baking soda and vinegar in a small bowl. Add to the creamed mixture.
- Mix the flour, salt, cinnamon and ginger together. Add to the creamed mixture and beat well.
- Shape by tablespoonfuls into balls. Place on a cookie sheet and flatten.
- Bake at 375 degrees until light brown.
- Cool on the cookie sheet for several minutes. Remove to a wire rack to cool completely.
- May sprinkle with sugar before baking but watch carefully to avoid burning.
- Yield: 48 servings.

Anna M. Carlson

Desserts

Bob and Bertha's
Favorite Oatmeal Cookies

*1 cup butter or margarine,
  softened*
½ cup sugar
1½ cups packed brown sugar
2 eggs
2 tablespoons milk
2 teaspoons vanilla extract
1¾ cups flour
1 teaspoon cinnamon
1 teaspoon salt
1 teaspoon baking soda
2½ cups rolled oats
1 cup chopped walnuts
1 cup chopped raisins

- Cream the butter, sugar and brown sugar in a mixer bowl until light and fluffy. Add the eggs, milk and vanilla and beat well.
- Sift the flour, cinnamon, salt and baking soda together. Add to the creamed mixture and beat well.
- Stir in the oats, walnuts and raisins. Drop by teaspoonfuls onto a greased cookie sheet.
- Bake at 350 degrees for 9 to 10 minutes or until light brown.
- Yield: 24 servings.

Anna M. Carlson

Desserts

West Tenth Avenue No-Bake Cookies

2 cups sugar
¼ cup baking cocoa
½ cup butter, softened
½ cup milk
1 cup peanut butter
1 tablespoon vanilla extract
2¾ to 3 cups rolled oats

- Cream the sugar, cocoa and butter in a mixer bowl until light and fluffy. Add the milk, peanut butter and vanilla and beat well. Stir in the oats, mixing well. Drop by spoonfuls onto waxed-paper-lined cookie sheets.
- Chill in the refrigerator until firm. Store in a covered container in the refrigerator.
- Yield: 36 servings.

Joy S. Harris

Desserts

Peanut Butter Cookies

1 cup packed brown sugar
1 cup sugar
1 cup shortening
2 eggs
1 teaspoon vanilla extract
1 cup peanut butter
3 cups flour
³/₄ teaspoon baking soda
¹/₂ teaspoon salt

- Cream the brown sugar, sugar and shortening in a mixer bowl until light and fluffy. Add the eggs, vanilla and peanut butter and beat well.
- Mix the flour, baking soda and salt together. Add to the creamed mixture and beat well.
- Shape by teaspoonfuls into balls and place on a cookie sheet. Flatten with a fork.
- Bake at 350 degrees for 10 to 12 minutes or until light brown.
- Cool on the cookie sheet for several minutes. Remove to a wire rack to cool completely.
- Yield: 36 servings.

Anna Hattie Vogl

Desserts

Sour Cream Cookies

1 cup sugar
$1/2$ cup shortening
$1/2$ cup sour cream
1 egg
1 teaspoon vanilla extract
$2^2/3$ cups flour
$1/2$ teaspoon salt
1 teaspoon baking powder
$1/2$ teaspoon nutmeg
$1/2$ teaspoon baking soda

- Cream the sugar and shortening in a mixer bowl until light and fluffy. Add the sour cream, egg and vanilla and beat well. Add the flour, salt, baking powder, nutmeg and baking soda and beat well.
- Chill, covered, for 30 minutes.
- Roll dough out to $1/4$-inch thickness on a floured surface. Cut into desired shapes with cookie cutters dipped in flour. Place on a cookie sheet.
- Bake at 425 degrees for 8 to 10 minutes or until light brown.
- Cool on the cookie sheet for several minutes. Remove to a wire rack to cool completely.
- Yield: 30 servings.

Elva LaCombe

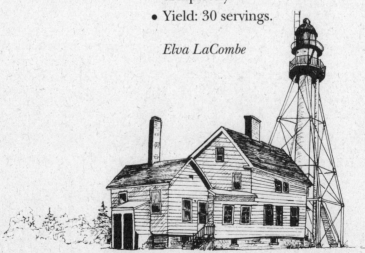

Desserts

Sugar Cookies

1½ cups sugar
1½ cups shortening
2 eggs
1 teaspoon vanilla extract
1 cup sour milk
4 cups (or more) flour
Pinch of salt
1 teaspoon baking soda
1½ teaspoons baking powder

- Cream the sugar and shortening in a mixer bowl until light and fluffy. Add the eggs, vanilla and sour milk and mix well.
- Mix the flour, salt, baking soda and baking powder together. Add to the creamed mixture. Chill, covered, for 2 hours or longer.
- Roll out the chilled cookie dough on a floured surface, adding enough flour to prevent sticking to the rolling pin. Cut with cookie cutters dipped in flour. Place on an ungreased cookie sheet.
- Bake at 375 degrees for 8 to 10 minutes or until light brown.
- Cool on the cookie sheet for several minutes. Remove to a wire rack to cool completely.
- Yield: 48 servings.

Mary Vogl Barber

Desserts

Thunder Bay Butter Tarts

1 recipe (3-crust) pie pastry
$\frac{1}{2}$ cup butter, softened
1 cup packed brown sugar
1 egg, beaten
$\frac{1}{2}$ teaspoon vanilla extract
$\frac{1}{2}$ cup currants, rinsed, dried
$\frac{1}{4}$ cup chopped pecans

- Roll out the pie pastry and cut into $2\frac{3}{4}$-inch circles. Place in greased muffin cups.
- Cream the butter and brown sugar in a mixer bowl until light and fluffy. Add the egg and vanilla and mix well. Stir in the currants and pecans. Fill each tart shell $\frac{3}{4}$ full.
- Bake at 425 degrees for 5 minutes. Reduce the oven temperature to 375 degrees. Bake for 10 to 12 minutes longer or until light brown.
- Cool in the pan for several minutes. Remove to a wire rack to cool completely.
- Yield: 12 servings.

Mary Harris

Desserts

Aunt Elva's Chocolate Cream Pie

1 cup sugar

$1/3$ cup flour or 3 tablespoons
  cornstarch

$1/4$ teaspoon salt

2 cups milk

2 (1-ounce) squares
  unsweetened chocolate,
  chopped

3 egg yolks, beaten

2 tablespoons butter

1 teaspoon vanilla extract

1 baked (9-inch) pie shell

• Combine the sugar, flour and salt in a saucepan and mix well. Add the milk gradually, mixing well. Stir in the chocolate. Cook over medium heat until the mixture boils, stirring constantly. Cook over low heat for 2 minutes, stirring constantly.

• Stir a small amount of the hot mixture into the egg yolks. Add the egg yolks to the hot mixture. Cook for 2 minutes longer, stirring constantly. Remove from the heat.

• Stir the butter and vanilla into the chocolate mixture, mixing well. Pour into the baked pie shell. Store in the refrigerator.

• Yield: 8 servings.

Elva LaCombe

Desserts

Aunt Elva's Lemon Meringue Pie

1 cup sugar
3 tablespoons cornstarch
3 tablespoons flour
Dash of salt
1½ cups hot water
3 egg yolks, slightly beaten
*2 tablespoons butter or
    margarine*
⅓ cup lemon juice
1 baked (9-inch) pie shell
1 recipe meringue

- Combine the sugar, cornstarch, flour and salt in a saucepan. Stir in the hot water until well mixed. Cook over high heat until the mixture comes to a boil, stirring constantly.
- Stir a small amount of the hot mixture into the egg yolks. Stir the egg yolks into the hot mixture.
- Reduce the heat. Cook over low heat for 2 minutes, stirring constantly. Stir in the butter and lemon juice until well mixed. Pour into the baked pie shell. Top with the meringue, sealing to the edge.
- Bake at 350 degrees until light brown.
- Yield: 8 servings.

Elva LaCombe

Desserts

Chocolate-Covered Peanut Butter Balls

3 (1-pound) packages
   confectioners' sugar
1 large jar peanut butter
3 tablespoons vanilla extract
1 pound semisweet chocolate
1 sheet paraffin wax

- Combine the confectioners' sugar, peanut butter and vanilla in a bowl and mix well. Shape into 1-inch balls. Chill in the refrigerator.
- Melt the chocolate and paraffin in the top of a double boiler over hot water. Dip the peanut butter balls into the chocolate to coat. Place on waxed paper. Let stand until the chocolate is set.
- May add chopped nuts to the chocolate mixture.
- Yield: 96 servings.

Jan M. Holt

Desserts

Cranberry Fudge

½ cup milk
2 cups sugar
¼ cup cream
3 tablespoons light corn syrup
½ teaspoon salt
1 tablespoon butter
1 teaspoon vanilla extract
½ cup fresh cranberries,
    chopped

- Butter the sides of a heavy 2-quart saucepan. Combine the milk, sugar, cream, corn syrup and salt in the saucepan. Cook over medium heat until the mixture boils, stirring frequently.
- Cook to 234 to 240 degrees on a candy thermometer, soft ball stage; remove from the heat and cool to lukewarm without stirring.
- Add the butter and vanilla. Beat until the candy is stiff and glossy. Stir in the cranberries. Pour into a buttered 8-inch square dish. Score while still warm. Cool completely and cut into squares.
- Yield: 30 servings.

Roxanne McKiddie

Desserts

Lighthouse Christmas Fudge

4¹/₂ cups sugar
Dash of salt
1 (12-ounce) can evaporated milk
2 tablespoons butter
3 bars German's sweet chocolate
2 cups chocolate chips
1 (13-ounce) jar marshmallow creme
2 cups chopped nuts

- Combine the sugar, salt, evaporated milk and butter in a saucepan. Cook over low heat for 6 minutes, stirring frequently.
- Place the sweet chocolate, chocolate chips, marshmallow creme and nuts in a large bowl. Pour the hot mixture into the bowl, stirring until the chocolate is melted. Pour into buttered pans. Cool and cut into squares.
- Yield: 24 servings.

Friend of The Shipwreck Society

Million-Dollar Fudge

4¹/₂ cups sugar
1 cup butter or margarine
1 cup evaporated milk
1 (14-ounce) jar marshmallow creme
2 cups chocolate chips

- Combine the sugar, butter and evaporated milk in a saucepan. Bring to a boil. Boil for 9 minutes, stirring frequently. Add the marshmallow creme and chocolate chips, stirring until melted.
- Pour into a large greased pan. Let stand until firm. Cut into squares.
- May add chopped nuts if desired.
- Yield: 30 servings.

Friend of The Shipwreck Society

Desserts

Peanut Brittle

2 cups sugar
½ cup hot water
1 cup light corn syrup
2 cups raw peanuts
1 tablespoon butter
1 teaspoon baking soda
1 teaspoon vanilla extract
¼ teaspoon salt

- Combine the sugar, hot water and corn syrup in a saucepan. Cook to 260 degrees on a candy thermometer. Add the peanuts and butter. Cook to 300 degrees on a candy thermometer, stirring constantly. Cook at 300 degrees for 2 to 3 minutes or just until the candy is golden brown, stirring constantly. Remove from the heat.
- Add the baking soda, vanilla and salt, stirring until foamy. Pour onto a large greased baking pan. Let stand until cool. Break into servings.
- Yield: 20 servings.

Friend of The Shipwreck Society

Desserts

No-Bake Skedaddles

3/4 cup sugar
2 tablespoons butter
1/2 cup evaporated milk
1 cup semisweet chocolate chips
2 cups chow mein noodles
1 cup miniature
  marshmallows

- Combine the sugar, butter and evaporated milk in a saucepan. Bring to a full rolling boil over high heat, stirring constantly. Remove from the heat. Add the chocolate chips, stirring until melted. Let stand for 15 minutes.
- Combine the chow mein noodles and marshmallows in a large bowl and mix well.
- Pour in the chocolate mixture, stirring until the noodles are coated. Drop by heaping teaspoonfuls onto a waxed-paper-lined cookie sheet.
- Chill for 1 hour or until set. Remove from the waxed paper.
- Yield: 36 servings.

Friend of The Shipwreck Society

Desserts

Pulled Taffy

3 cups sugar
1/2 cup vinegar
1 to 2 tablespoons butter
1/2 cup water
1 teaspoon vanilla extract
1/2 teaspoon baking soda

- Combine the sugar, vinegar, butter and water in a saucepan. Cook over medium heat to 300 to 310 degrees on a candy thermometer, hard-crack stage.
- Stir in the vanilla and baking soda. Pour onto a buttered plate. Turn in the edges. Let stand until cool enough to handle. Pull with buttered hands until white and brittle. Cut into bite-size pieces with buttered scissors.
- Yield: 12 servings.

Friend of The Shipwreck Society

Desserts

Index

Index

Index

Index

Great Lakes Shipwreck Historical Society, Inc.
111 Ashmun Street
Sault Ste. Marie, Michigan 49783
(800) 635-1742

Please send me _____ copies of *Treasured Recipes from the Shipwreck Coast*
@ $14.95 each $_____
add postage and handling @ $ 3.50 each $_____
Total $_____

❑ Check   ❑ MasterCard   ❑ VISA

Card No._____

Expiration Date _____ Signature _____

Name _____ Phone (____) _____

Address _____

City _____ State _____ Zip _____

Please make checks payable to Great Lakes Shipwreck Historical Society, Inc.

Great Lakes Shipwreck Historical Society, Inc.
111 Ashmun Street
Sault Ste. Marie, Michigan 49783
(800) 635-1742

Please send me _____ copies of *Treasured Recipes from the Shipwreck Coast*
@ $14.95 each $_____
add postage and handling @ $ 3.50 each $_____
Total $_____

❑ Check   ❑ MasterCard   ❑ VISA

Card No._____

Expiration Date _____ Signature _____

Name _____ Phone (____) _____

Address _____

City _____ State _____ Zip _____

Please make checks payable to Great Lakes Shipwreck Historical Society, Inc.

Order Form